THE CONFIDENT YEARS: CANADA IN THE 1920s

ROBERT J. BONDY
Sir Frederick Banting Secondary School

WILLIAM C. MATTYS
Sir Frederick Banting Secondary School

PRENTICE-HALL OF CANADA, LTD., SCARBOROUGH, ONTARIO

Contents

A GROWING MATERIAL ABUNDANCE

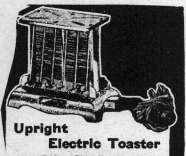

"With another 350 000 families installing electricity for the first time in the 1920s, seven of every ten homes in Canada had electric power by 1930."

A. B. Hodgetts, *Decisive Decades*, p. 312

Electrical Gifts, 1929	
Dishwasher	$145.00
Egg Cooker	3.00
Hair Dryer	11.50
Ironing Machine	135.50
Refrigerator	150.00
Table Lamp	2.50
Electric Range	160.00

Ontario Hydro, 1929

Queenston hydro-electric power house

Alternatives to Electric Appliances	
Windmill	$60.
Wood or coal cook-stove	40-70.
3 Burner oil stove	28.
4 Burner gas range	38.
Hand washing machine	19.

The Greater Canada of Tomorrow

"Every day is bringing some marvellous new application of electricity into the making of which have gone years of research and experiments.... The prospects for the application of our water power are boundless. After Norway, Canada has the greatest per capita water power development, yet only 8½% of Canada's power resources are now used. It is one of the mighty factors in building up the greater Canada of tomorrow—the Canada of industrial achievement and enterprise."

Northern Electric, 1926

Maclean's Magazine, Oct. 15, 1925

Commode Chair

63-300 Adult's Commode Chair, hardwood, in Golden finish. Shaped top slat; large seat with lid. Commode box has door on side. Price........ **5.00**

Improved Electric Iron

01-511. EATONIA Iron with improved back rest, is heavily nickel-plated; well-shaped, evenly-heated base; in domestic size. A worthy member of our "Good Value" family. Price **3.50**

Ford Model A assembly line

Takes one and one-half times first-class freight rate.
143.50
WITH POLE

IMPERIAL DEMOCRAT

This is a Democrat built for Western conditions. Made strong where democrats first go wrong. Heavy axles, sturdy springs, gear of selected hickory, steel reinforced, braced and bolted at all points of heavy strain. A Democrat that is giving splendid satisfaction. Of very powerful build and superior design, and a wonderful democrat value.

SEE ITS SPLENDID CONSTRUCTION

Gear—1½-inch axles, triple elliptic front spring, and two 4-plate, 1⅜-inch rear springs. **Wheels**—1⅛-inch tread, high-grade hickory wheels, with double riveted rims. Front wheels 38 inches and rear wheels 42 inches high. **Body**—7 feet 4 inches by 31½ inches; sheet-iron-edged box, with large and roomy seats and high metal dash. **Pole**—2¼-inch hickory, correctly shaped. Complete with whiffletrees and neckyoke. **Finish**—Painted in glossy **Black** with **Dark Green** gears.

437M-346. Imperial Democrat with Pole. No Shafts. Weight 675 lbs. Price........ **143.50**

437M-347. Imperial Democrat with Shafts. No Pole. Weight 650 lbs. Price........ **138.75**

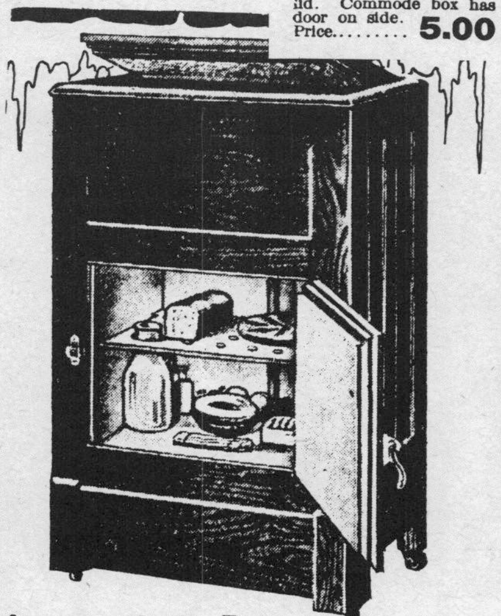

Inexpensively Priced

63-100 Though built on correct principles and well constructed, this refrigerator is priced very moderately. Made of hardwood, kiln-dried, finished **Golden** color; walls are thoroughly insulated, producing cold, dry temperature at low cost of ice. Ice rack is made of galvanized iron and is removable; cleanable flues; metal provision shelf with accommodation for quart milk bottle. Outside measurements: width 23¼ ins.; depth 16¼ ins.; height 39¼ ins. Fitted with casters. (Refrigerator only). Price.......... **12.50**

63-101 Similar to 63-100, but **interior of provision chamber in white enamel finish.** **14.50**

63-002 Similar Refrigerator to 63-100, but of larger capacity. Outside measurements are: width 26¼ ins.; depth 18¼ ins.; height 41¼ ins. Fitted with casters. Price.......... **16.25**

63-003 Similar to 63-002, but **interior of provision chamber in white enamel finish.** **18.50**

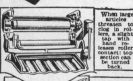

Acme
The Safe Washer
When large articles threaten to clog in rollers, a slight tap with hand releases roller contact: top section can be turned back.
Wringer swinglocks and sets at any angle enabling you to place a second tub where most convenient.
The oscillating (to and fro) movement swishes the clothes thoroughly, washing without injury to finest fabrics.
New style corrugated, drain board is of aluminum.
98.00

State name of Company supplying your power and w... require 25 or 60-cycle motor. We do not supply motor for di...

The Acme Electric is a Thorough Worker and Most Reliable

MADE according to the best washing principles, the "Acme" is ... help in the home; and you could not find a more reliable, bett... though you paid a much higher price. Let this dependable Wash... the drudgery of wash-day. At this low price you cannot afford to ...

Because we sell this machine to you direct, you profit by a ... saving and secure a Washer that is high-grade in every detail—s... thoroughly practical and safe and easy to use.

Tub is made of Planished Hard Rolled Copper, tinned inside. It has a capacity of about seven sheets. Metal is all die drawn, and no square corners are left to catch and hold dirt. You can wipe out inside of tub as clean as you would a dish. The large "Splasher" or "Rubber" inside the tub assists greatly in the operation of washing. Tub is movable and can be lifted out.

Frame is constructed of 1¼-inch angle steel, firmly riveted together, and reinforced with heavy, drawn steel corners.

All Machinery is contained in one solid cast-iron column, and there is not a wheel exposed.

Motor is ¼-horsepower, ... and fully guaranteed. ... nected to machine by a la... and-canvas" endless bel... nection between motor ... tively prevents any short... it impossible to receive ... while operating the machi...

Wringer has all-metal f... 12-inch solid rubber roller... working safety release. ... positive stop at any nece... you will find a wonderful ... desiring to wring from o... without moving the mach...

13-500 Acme Electric Washer, described above.
Price..

(See note under illustration regarding Motor accompanying W...

Without Attachments 32.50

The "EMPIRE" Electric Vacuum Cleaner

97-8205 In this **Cleaner** exceptional power has been combined with simplicity, convenience, dependability and beauty. The high speed motor produces a tremendous suction which easily and quickly collects the dirt embedded in the rugs. This cleaner also takes the stubborn clinging surface litter, such as thread and lint, which is done by means of its patented broom-action brush, a device easily slipped over the nozzle when wanted. Six attachments enable you to remove every particle of dust and dirt ordinarily hard to reach and difficult to clean with duster or broom. Fibre handle with comfortable pistol grip, fitted with trigger switch. Complete with six attachments. Price.......... **37.50**

Complete Set With Six Attachments.

"Acme A" Coal Annex

17.50

No more necessity for cold kitchens, if your gas or electric stove is fitted with one of these handy little heaters! It develops an amazing amount of heat for its small size—enough to keep the kitchen warm and comfortable, and do a surprising amount of cooking besides.

The "ACME A" Annex is 26 ins. deep by 14 ins. wide, and may be set to the exact level of your cooking stove by means of adjustable legs.

Cooking Top is 25½ x 13½ ins., and fitted with two No. 8 size cooking covers.

Firepot is 16 ins. long, 6 ins. wide, and 10 ins. deep, lined with brick, and fitted with heavy, duplex shaker grates. Special flue construction utilizes all the heat generated. Fire door and ashpit (with slide damper), are nickel-plated.

15-119 "ACME A" Coal Annex. Shipped from foundry.
Price.......................... **17.50**

01-523. Everbright Lamp, for general home use; burns gasoline and air; safe and economical. Base nickel-plated. White shade 10 ins. in diameter, two mantles, pump, wrench, hanger, cleaning pick and extra generator included. Has underwriters' approval **10.95**

AN EASY WORKING CISTERN PUMP

IMPERIAL PITCHER-SPOUT, OPEN BASE CISTERN PUMP

For Wells or Cisterns up to 20 feet Deep

The extra long cylinder gives greater capacity for pumping; has highly polished iron cylinder. Entire pump is made of highest grade cast-iron.

441L-706. 3-Inch Cistern Pump, for 1¼-Inch Pipe. Pump only. Weight 25 lbs. Price.......... **2.85**

441L-707. 3½-Inch Cistern Pump, for 1¼-Inch Pipe. Pump only. Weight 30 lbs. Price.......... **3.45**

441L-708. 4-Inch Cistern Pump, for 1½-Inch Pipe. Pump only. Weight 35 lbs. Price.......... **4.25**

Takes third-class freight rate.

Order this from Regina, Saskatoon or Winnipeg

All items were taken from *Eaton's Catalogues*, 1927

TO BUY

Influenza . . .
The Unseen Passenger
in *Your* Car

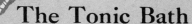

MANY a long winter illness starts from a seemingly harmless motor drive. Drafts swish through the car. Your body becomes cold and shivery. Result: Influenza—or worse!

Guard against winter driving ills. Guard against them by wearing Penmans 95—Canada's famous health underwear. Penmans 95 gives maximum winter protection—yet is never too hot for indoor wear. It is springy and resilient—absorbs perspiration—the most durable and sanitary quality underwear you can buy.

Made in all the most popular styles and lengths for men, women and children.

PENMANS 95

Is a fine light-weight garment famous both for its remarkable wearing qualities and health protection. Made of fine selected yarns that increase softness, minimize shrinkage and insure exceptional durability.

Write for free set of Penmans exercises—an invaluable aid to health and robust physical development.

Penmans
HEALTH UNDERWEAR

Halifax Herald, Oct. 24, 1929

Never Mind!
Smoke a REX

2 "Poker Hands" in the new 25c package

Manitoba Free Press, Aug. 25, 1927

The Tonic Bath

It is decidedly a gain to find a soap that makes the bath a refreshing delight. It is decidedly a boon to find in that soap a health bringer as well. That is the double benefit you gain with

LIFEBUOY HEALTH SOAP

To a soap base of the utmost purity we add a gentle disinfectant agent that makes the skin "glow with health". The healing, copious lather of Lifebuoy thoroughly cleanses the pores and leaves them disinfected and sweet.

The mild Lifebuoy odour quickly vanishes after use. All grocers sell Lifebuoy.

LEVER BROTHERS LIMITED
TORONTO   17

Maclean's Magazine, June 1, 1920

Keeping the pores open and CLEANSED with Lifebuoy means a healthy skin.

Are we really happy?

Here is a gripping story of a woman who thought the world owed her happiness, and when it seemed to be within her grasp . . . . but you must read—"THE GIRL WHO WANTED HAPPINESS" in the SEPTEMBER TRUE STORY MAGAZINE!

The purpose of TRUE STORY MAGAZINE is not to preach, yet, in the sense that this great magazine reveals the truth about life, every one of its stories is a powerful sermon. Just as the Minister, through his broad sympathy and deep understanding, seeks to guide his people into the ways of righteous living and happiness, so do the true life chronicles of TRUE STORY MAGAZINE send out their messages of hope, inspiration and encouragement to the millions of readers who make up its vast audience.

Manitoba Free Press, Aug. 5, 1927

[**FREE**—Send for Two Trial Packages]

He's *young* to be holding a job like that!

SALES MANAGER at . . . Bert Johnson *is* young . . . a position. But from the . . . began his business caree . . . moved quickly.

Good health has always bee . . . —good health promoted by . . . —giving him the proper nouris . . . for a keen mind and an energ . . . hard-working body. Right food . . . mean a great deal to you, too. Part . . . ularly Grape-Nuts. It sur . . . delightfully appetizing f . . . essential elements of nutrition . . .

Nourishment Like This Puts You Ahead!

Grape=Nuts
for Delicious Nourishment

Manitoba Free Press, Aug. 9, 1927

TALK OF THE TWENTIES

"Not more than 5 or 6 years ago if an airplane succeeded in landing at your town without cracking up in somebody's pasture, everyone turned out to see the strange contraption.

"A few of the really bold folk would go up [in the plane], provided they were willing to spend the necessary $5-$10. Those were the good old days for barnstorming and let us say that we owe a great deal to the barnstormers, most of them for introducing flying to countless thousands of people under conditions calling for utmost resourcefulness and good piloting.

Canadian Aviation Magazine, 1933

SLANG OF THE ERA

cat's meow	– very sharp
berries	– the best
swell	– marvellous
big cheese	– big shot, a prominent person
all wet	– out to lunch
bee's knees	– wonderful person
scram	– leave in a hurry
flat tire	– dull personality
giggle water	– booze
gin mill	– illegal still
blind pig	– illegal drinking spot
speakeasy	– illegal drinking spot
gatecrashers	– police raid on speakeasy
hi Jack!	– thief's greeting to a rumrunner
hooch	– booze
splifficated, ossified	– drunk
dogs	– shoes
lamps	– eyes
cheaters	– eyeglasses
raz-ma-taz	– restless vigour
struggle buggy	– a car for courting
upchuck	– to throw up
applesauce	– nonsense
baloney	– nonsense
bunk	– nonsense
banana oil	– nonsense
horse feathers	– nonsense
heebie jeebies	– the jitters
hep	– wise, "with it"
keen	– attractive
kidda	– a friendly form of address
ritzy, swanky	– elegant
the real McCoy	– genuine article
smeller	– nose
spiffy	– fashionable

Hijinks and practical jokes frequently provided much humour among friends during the 1920s.

JOKES

Tin Lizzie Joke

A farmer tears the tin roof off his barn and mails it to Ford. A week later the company writes:

"Your Model T is the worst wreck we've ever seen; it will take us two weeks to fix it."

R. Collins, *A Great Way To Go*, p. 49

SPEAKER (AT A PROHIBITION MEETING)

"A friend of mine purchased a barrel of liquor and drank himself to death before it was a quarter gone. Are there any comments on this sad incident?"

Silence, then from the back of the house – "Where's the rest of it?"

As Mrs. ____ tossed to and fro in her bed one night, the clock struck three, and a voice of a little child came plaintively from a crib:

"Mama!" it said.

"Yes, love?"

"Mama, I can't sleep, won't you please tell me a fairy story?"

"Wait, my love," said Mrs. ____ , "your father will soon be home and he will tell us both one."

NUBS OF NEWS

Gas Tax

Alberta—1922—$.02 per gal
Manitoba—1923—$.01 per gal
Ontario—1925—$.03 per gal

Driver's License
Ontario – 1927, Operators
P.E.I. – None required

Total number of automobiles in 3 leading nations in 1925:

U.S.A. 3 735 171

Britain 1 510 000

Canada 652 121

Number of persons per automobile in 3 leading nations in 1925:

Canada 14

Britain 24

U.S.A. 31

WIT, WISDOM, AND WHIMSY

"For the man who still walks, there is one joy left in life. He doesn't have to jump every time a boost in the price of gasoline is announced." *Saskatoon Star, 1920*

"People would be a lot better off if they cared as much about heaven's opinion as the neighbours'." *Calgary Morning Albertan, 1920*

"Jazz is reported to be dying. There's no other way to account for the strange noise it makes." *Saskatoon Phoenix, 1920*

"At any rate, the use of cigarettes will never become common among the women who darn stockings." *Kingston British Whig, 1920.*

"The men who bring up large families these days deserve credit, and many of them could not get along without it." *Vancouver Province, 1920.*

"Police are still hunting bootleggers. Most everybody else seems to have found theirs." *Elmira Signet, 1925.*

"Especially dangerous are the rum-running motorists who run with the rum inside of them." *Toronto Globe, 1920.*

"What with the low-neck gowns, short skirts, cobweb stockings and half hose, doctors will have to vaccinate on the ear." *Cobalt Nugget, 1920.*

"Lack of wind forced postponement of the Fisher Cup Yacht Race at Toronto yesterday. They will never have to call off an election for this reason." *Hamilton Spectator, 1925.*

"There is a telephone to every eight persons in Canada and judging from reports of 'Lines Busy' the other seven are on the wire every time you want to use yours." *Hespeller Herald, 1920. Maclean's Magazine, 1920-1925*

Radio Listening

This farm housewife in southern Alberta may be a bit inconvenienced by her radio headphones if she has to move to hang up clothes. Most listeners of the wireless or radio "miracle" didn't take it quite so casually. Especially in the early 1920s, radio fans called "twiddlers" would, for long hours every evening, adjust and re-adjust a crystal set and a "cat's whisker" to pull in distant radio signals. By the mid 1920s, battery-powered radios such as the one shown were common across Canada. By Christmas 1928, the public could buy a plug-in, electric current, and multi-tube Rogers-Majestic, General Electric, Philco, and Atwater-Kent radios connected to a loudspeaker. By the end of the decade, such new radios in their handsome wooden stand-up cabinets were a normal part of Canada's living rooms and no longer amazed people.

A woman washes while listening to the radio, Calgary area, 1922.

Radio Coverage

"While the new-fangled radio received a great deal of attention and sales, not many Canadians could receive Canadian radio signals. Canada's total radio-station power output was 50 kilowatts, compared to 6 800 kilowatts for American stations. With more than one third of Canada's radio signal power centred in Toronto and Montreal, great isolated areas were served only or mainly by the high-powered radio stations from the United States." *E. A. Weir, The Struggle for National Broadcasting in Canada, p. 83*

The telephone operator was a social institution in most communities. To place a telephone call, the caller spoke directly with the operator. In many communities, people called the operator by name, and she knew much of the news in the surrounding area.

HUMAN FLIES

As buildings such as Montreal's Sun Life Building, and Toronto's Royal York reached heights of 25 storeys or more, daredevils began to thrill spectators by climbing up the skyscrapers.

INFORMATION

"Canada has one telephone for every eleven people. This percentage is surpassed by only one other country." *Northern Electric, 1925*

Agnes Macphail was born in 1890 in Grey County, Ontario. She took a keen interest in politics, and was an organizer for the United Farmers of Ontario. Macphail ran for office in 1921 and, at age 31, became the first female member of the House of Commons, She was interested in helping the sick, the handicapped, and prisoners. In a long political career, Agnes Macphail fought for women's rights and pioneered much social welfare legislation.

Dateline: Ottawa, House of Commons, 1925

"I believe it is the desire, Mr. Speaker, of everyone in this House that the home should be preserved. I believe the preservation of the home as an institution in the future lies almost entirely in the hands of the men. If they are willing to give to women economic freedom within that home, if they are willing to live by the standard that they wish the women to live by, the home will be preserved. If the preservation of the home means the enslavement of women, economically or morally, then we had better break it.... So, when we have a single standard for men and women, both morally and economically, we shall have a home that is well worth preserving."

Agnes Macphail, Feb. 26, 1925

AGNES MACPHAIL

Dateline: Toronto, 1923

Cure for Diabetes Proven Successful

A team of physicians led by Dr. F. C. Banting has confirmed that Banting's discovery of insulin is effective in the cure and treatment of diabetes. The testing showed that the insulin treatment can restore body weight to the diabetic and control diabetic coma.

FREDERICK BANTING

Frederick Banting received his medical training at the University of Toronto. After serving in the First World War, he opened a private practice in London, Ontario. He later joined the research department at the University of Toronto's Faculty of Medicine, where he conducted extensive experiments and finally succeeded in isolating insulin. He was aided in his research by Charles H. Best. Frederick Banting's long years of research were recognized with a Nobel Prize in 1923.

STEPHEN LEACOCK

Stephen Leacock was born in Hampshire, England. His family came to Canada in the nineteenth century and settled on a farm near Lake Simcoe in Ontario. He was educated at Upper Canada College and the University of Toronto, graduating in 1899. He went on to complete graduate studies in economics and politics at the University of Chicago. Leacock became a staff member at McGill University and eventually Head of the Department of Political Science and Economics. At McGill, he wrote and published a number of scholarly papers in political science. However, it was not for his research studies in political science that he became famous, but his ability to make Canadians laugh. In his lifetime, Stephen Leacock became Canada's leading humourist. His reputation was world-wide and his books were published in many countries.

Stephen Leacock was a prodigous writer—*Literary Lapses* (1910), *Nonsense Novels* (1911), *Arcadian Adventures with the Idle Rich* (1914), *College Days* (1923), *Winnowed Wisdom* (1926), *Laugh with Leacock* (1930), were translated into many languages. His *Sunshine Sketches of a Little Town* (1912), with such memorable characters as Dean Drone and Mr. Pupkin, became popular reading during the twenties. Leacock was also a wonderful storyteller and he was in demand for lectures and readings from his works. Some of this writing was done in Leacock's summer home in Orillia and the community has purchased this home to be used as a museum.

Howie Morenz   Al Plunkett   Emily Carr   Albert Belanger   Marie Dressler   "Wop" May

HEADLINERS:
PERSONALITIES OF THE 1920s

LIONEL CONACHER

Lionel "Big Train" Conacher is Canada's all-round athlete of the half-century. He grew up in Toronto during the 1920s, where, at an early age, he participated in many sports. He was a boxer and a wrestler, and won championship titles in both fields. Conacher played baseball for the Toronto Maple Leafs and lacrosse for the Toronto Maitlands. As a hockey defenceman he played for the Pittsburg Pirates, the New York Americans, the Chicago Black Hawks, and the Montreal Maroons. However, he demonstrated his greatest skill and versatility as a halfback for the Toronto Argonauts.

Dateline: Toronto, 1921

ARGOS WIN GREY CUP

The Toronto Argos defeat the Edmonton Eskimos 23-0 in the Grey Cup. An individual record was set when Lionel Conacher scored 15 points. Conacher was a one-man team as he displayed his running and kicking skill.

PILOT DICKENS SENDS MESSAGE

"PUNCH" DICKENS

Winnipeg. Oct. 8.—"No trace of the McAlpine party." This six-word sentence, flashed out of the North after five days of silent suspense, prefaces a modest resume of Pilot "Punch" Dickens' second reckless "dash" to the Arctic circle. And it is an epitome of the futile efforts of an airplane armada to locate Col. C. D. H. McAlpine and his seven fellow explorers who faded into the barrens one month ago today.

Twice within two weeks the 20-year-old Edmonton airman has plunged through the rock-strewn tundras to the northern coast of Canada. His first flight took him from northern Alberta to Coronation Gulf and back again in an effort to check up on the lost men. Late last night came word of a new sortie, covering one thousand miles across the depth and through the midst of the Northwest Territories to Bathurst Inlet and return.

This morning Dickens rested at Fort Smith on the north Alberta boundary, after having casually suggested to search officials that he might hop off today on a dash via Fort Rae, on Great Slave Lake, to the mouth of the Coppermine River, a matter of at least 12,000 miles of flying. His next search move, however, will be to proceed to Stoney Rapids base in north Saskatchewan, where his machine will be equipped with skis. It is probable that he will first return to McMurray on the Athabasca river, in northern Alberta, according to Western Canada Airways authorities. *Hamilton Spectator*, Oct. 8, 1929

Clennell H. "Punch" Dickens was a First World War air ace and northern bush pilot. He was born in 1899 at Portage la Prairie, Manitoba. During the 1920s Dickens captured the public's attention with his daring, record-breaking flights in Canada's North. He and other pilots like him helped open up the North and make it accessible.

Mazo de la Roche   J. S. Woodsworth   J. W. Dafoe   Mary Pickford   Lucy Maud Montgomery

OUR ROYAL
PRINCE.
Finest Bicycle you would
want to own.
Fully Guaranteed.

The Liquor Balance

Costs	Benefits
1. Canada's drink bill.	1. The liquor revenue.
2. Drink-caused idleness.	
3. Misdirected labour.	
4. Drink-caused mortality.	
5. The waste of grain.	
6. Charitable outlay caused by drinking.	
7. Crime and drunkenness.	F. S. Spence, *The Campaign Manual,*

PRESERVING THE

Burford, Ontario, Home and School Association, 1921

BOYS ARE TOO WARM GIRLS ARE TOO COLD

Lightness of Apparel Worn By Girl Students Requires Furnace Stoking

Boys with Heavy Clothes Complain of the Heat

Because of the lightness of the clothing worn by the collegiate girl students, a serious heating problem has presented itself in the local high schools. This was the admission today of an official, who states that real difficulty is encountered in the regulation of the temperature to a degree where it is comfortable for both girl and boy students.

By reason of the light clothes the girls wear in the fall and winter, as well as spring, a high degree of heat is required to keep the room sufficiently warm enough for them, while at the same time it is too hot for the boys garbed in more substantial clothing. What is to be done in the matter is puzzling school officials. If the classrooms are made warm enough for the girls the temperature is too high to be comfortable for the young men, it was explained.

At the same time that this unusual situation is revealed comes the statement from Mrs. J. I. A. Hunt, chairman of the board, that all collegiate girls should be attired in regulation uniforms. Her statement followed indirect complaints made by residents living near collegiates over the scanty clothing worn by collegiate girls.

The chairman herself frowns on the sleeveless dresses, short skirts and low-cut necks, representing the styles of dresses worn by the high school girls.

She added that there could be no denying the scantiness of the attire of the teen-age collegiate girls and that was one of her principal reasons for wanting uniforms introduced into the collegiates.

London Free Press, October 17, 1929

TEACHER'S CONTRACT

This is an agreement between Miss Lottie Jones, teacher and the Board of Education of the Middletown School, thereby Miss Lottie Jones agrees to teach in the Middletown School for a period of eight months beginning September 1, 1923. The Board of Education agrees to pay Miss Lottie Jones the sum of seventy-five dollars (75) per month.

Miss Lottie Jones agrees:

1. Not to get married. This contract becomes null and void immediately if the teacher marries.

2. Not to keep company with men.

3. To be at home between the hours of 8 p.m. and 6 a.m. unless she is in attendance at a school function.

4. Not to loiter downtown in ice cream parlors.

5. Not to leave town at any time without the permission of the Chairman of the Board of Trustees.

6. Not to smoke cigarettes. This contract becomes null and void immediately if the teacher is found smoking.

7. Not to drink beer, wine or whiskey. This contract becomes null and void immediately if the teacher is found drinking beer, wine or whiskey.

8. Not to ride in a carriage or automobile with any man except her brothers or father.

9. Not to dress in bright colors.

10. Not to dye her hair.

11. To wear at least two petticoats.

12. Not to wear dresses more than two inches above the ankle.

13. To keep the schoolroom clean: to sweep the classroom floor at least once daily; to scrub the classroom floor once a week with hot water and soap; to clean the blackboards at least once daily; to start the fire at 7 a.m. so that the room will be warm at 8 a.m. when the children arrive; to carry out the ashes at least once daily.

14. Not to use face powder, mascara or paint the lips.

Church at Baie St. Paul, near Rivière du Loup, Quebec, 1929

CAREFUL WAYS

ALCOHOL GRIPS THE WORLD

National Woman's Christian Temperance Union, Evanston, Illinois

"Well, to my mind, drinking, smoking, dancing, shooting pool, watching indecent films and buying frivolous clothes are a waste of time and money. On the surface, some of these activities appear harmless enough, but in time they can lead an individual down the road to physical and moral ruin."
A Concerned Citizen

SUNDAY LAWS

In Force in the Province of Ontario

PROHIBIT

1. LABOR. With certain exceptions this includes:

(a) THE WORK OF LABORERS, MECHANICS and MANUFACTURERS.

(b) ALL FARM WORK, such as SEEDING, HARVESTING, FENCING, DITCHING.

(c) WORK ON RAILWAYS, such as BUILDING and CONSTRUCTION, and also REPAIR WORK, except in emergencies, and TRAFFIC, excepting the forwarding of PASSENGER AND CERTAIN FREIGHT TRAINS.

(d) ALL BUILDING, TEAMING, DRIVING FOR BUSINESS PURPOSES, THE WORK OF BAKERS AND BARBERS, Etc.

(e) THE WORK OF MUSICIANS AND PAID PERFORMERS OF ANY KIND. Works of necessity and mercy excepted.

2. BUSINESS. It is unlawful to MAKE CONTRACTS or to BUY, SELL or DELIVER ANYTHING on Sunday, including LIQUORS, CIGARS, NEWSPAPERS, Etc. Generally speaking the only exceptions are DELIVERING PASSENGERS' BAGGAGE, MILK for domestic use, and SUPPLYING MEALS AND MEDICINES.

3. ALL GAMES, RACES OR OTHER SPORTS FOR MONEY OR PRIZES, or which are noisy, or at which a fee is charged, and the business of AMUSEMENT or ENTERTAINMENT.

4. ALL EXCURSIONS for hire and with the object of pleasure, by TRAIN, STEAMER or OTHER CONVEYANCE.

5. ADVERTISING in Canada, unlawful things to take place on Sunday, either in Canada or across the line.

6. IMPORTING, SELLING or DISTRIBUTING FOREIGN NEWSPAPERS on Sunday.

7. ALL GAMBLING, TIPPLING, USING PROFANE LAN-GUAGE, and all other acts which disturb the public quiet.

8. ALL PUBLIC MEETINGS, except in Churches.

9. HUNTING, SHOOTING, FISHING; also BATHING in any public place or in sight of a place of public worship, or private residence.

THE PENALTY IS FROM $1.00 TO $500.00

THE GAME LAW

Of the Province makes Sunday a CLOSE SEASON for all GAME and HUNTING and SHOOTING UNLAWFUL on that day.

THE PENALTY IS FROM $5.00 TO $25.00

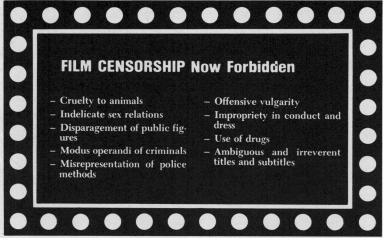

FILM CENSORSHIP Now Forbidden

- Cruelty to animals
- Indelicate sex relations
- Disparagement of public figures
- Modus operandi of criminals
- Misrepresentation of police methods
- Offensive vulgarity
- Impropriety in conduct and dress
- Use of drugs
- Ambiguous and irreverent titles and subtitles

Maclean's Magazine, Nov. 1, 1925

LORD'S DAY ACT, CANADA

". . . . is intended to prevent the open shop, the exploitations of the public by organizers of excursions . . . and also the opening of places of public amusement for which a fee is charged. Legitimate recreation and amusement are in no way interfered with."

Charles Fitzpatrick, Minister of Justice, Canada, 1906

SUNDAY CUSTOMS

Some families did all of their manual domestic labour, such as baking and shining shoes, on Saturday evening. For many households, Sunday meant morning and evening church service, social visits, and little physical exertion.

THE FAMILY

Picnicking at Little Arm, Saskatchewan, 1920

Winter fun for the family in Montreal

Father was still the head of the household. Although many more women held jobs in the 1920s than ever before, the man was still the major wage-earner. The father drove the family car (1 out of every 2 Canadian families had a car by 1928), and organized the increasing number of family vacations. It was still part of his role to discipline the children, although this task was becoming increasingly more difficult. The strict moral codes of the Victorian era were being replaced by a greater freedom for the young.

JALNA

Mazo de la Roche

ANNE OF GREEN GABLES

Lucy Maud Montgomery

SUNSHINE SKETCHES OF A LITTLE TOWN

Stephen Leacock

THE SONGS OF A SOURDOUGH

Robert Service

"By the sea, by the sea, by the beautiful sea", Prince Edward Island, 1928

This family has pitched their tent at a municipal motor camp, near Ottawa, Ontario

CANADA'S POPULATION								
	1921	1922	1923	1924	1925	1926	1927	1928
Prince Edward Island	88 615	88 400	88 020	87 700	87 300	87 000	86 700	86 400
Nova Scotia	523 837	527 100	530 000	533 600	536 900	540 000	543 000	547 000
New Brunswick	387 876	391 700	395 500	399 400	403 300	407 200	411 000	415 000
Quebec	2 361 199	2 400 000	2 439 000	2 480 000	2 520 000	2 561 800	2 604 000	2 647 000
Ontario	2 933 662	2 976 000	3 019 000	3 062 000	3 103 000	3 145 600	3 187 000	3 229 000
Manitoba	610 118	615 600	621 200	626 800	632 400	639 056	647 000	655 000
Saskatchewan	757 510	770 600	783 700	796 800	809 900	820 738	836 000	851 000
Alberta	588 454	592 200	595 900	599 600	603 300	607 599	617 000	631 900
British Columbia	524 582	535 000	544 000	553 000	560 300	568 400	575 000	583 000
Yukon	4 157	3 800	3 600	3 550	3 500	3 450	3 470	3 500
Northwest Territories	7 988	8 150	8 320	8 490	8 600	8 850	9 050	9 200
Canada	8 788 483	8 908 550	9 028 240	9 150 940	9 268 700	9 389 693	9 519 220	9 658 000

Canada Year Book, 1928

Household Bills

1 ton [907.2 kg] coal	$16.37
1 cord° of hardwood	14.48
1 gallon [4.5 litres] coal oil	
6 room house with modern conveniences, rent per month	27.49
6 room house with incomplete modern conveniences, rent per month	19.69
3 min phone talk, London [Ontario] to Toronto	.70

°no metric equivalent

The most dramatic change was in the role of the mother. It was an easier task in the 1920s to organize the home because the cluttered Victorian style at the turn of the century had given way to simpler and more compact designs. The widespread use of electricity revolutionized home appliances and reduced work. The woman no longer had to stoke the fire in the kitchen stove and clean out the ashes. She could get water from the kitchen sink instead of fetching it from an outdoor pump. Corner stores offered a greater variety of convenience foods which made meal preparation a more pleasant task.

$32.50

$6 000
Six-room solid brick, complete basement. Side drive; fine lots with fruit trees.

$7 000
Well-built brick; 4 bedrooms; large porch; 3 piece bath; good cellar; furnace; electric features. Good alley at side and lots of room for car.

$7 800
Large living room with fireplace, dining room with beamed ceiling, kitchen with built-in cabinets, four large bedrooms, 3 piece bathroom – hot water heated.

A modern urban home

SHOPPING LIST

1 kg sugar	$ .18
1 kg coffee	1.35
1 kg tea	1.60
1 kg salt	.08
1 kg cheese	.71
1 kg bread	.17
1 kg flour	.12
1 kg sirloin steak	.68
1 kg pork	.58
1 kg bacon	.93
1 kg ham	1.32
1 kg butter	.95
1 kg potatoes	.04
1 can tomatoes	.16
1 can peas	.17
1 can corn	.16
1 l milk	.04
1 bushel° apples	.27

° No metric equivalent

$35.50

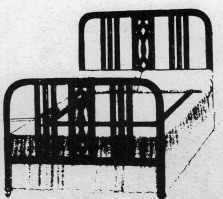

$16.50

$42.25

$28.00

All items were taken from *Eaton's Catalogues*, 1925-1927.

"EVERY WOMAN SHOULD

FEW OPENINGS FOR GIRLS
in biscuit and candy departments.
8-HOUR DAY.
WAGES FOR BEGINNERS $5.50
PER WEEK.
APPLY McCORMICK MFG. CO.
E25h

London Free Press, May 28, 1919

CANADA'S SUMMER GIRL

GOES TO
MUSKOKA
LA BAIE DE CHALEUR
PRINCE EDWARD ISLAND
ST. JOHN RIVER VALLEY
NOVA SCOTIA - BY -
THE SEA

via **The National Way**

OR
NIPIGON
QUETICO
MINAKI

OUT OF
LOWER ST...
MARITIM...

QUEBE...
NOR...

PR...
PA...

FREE COPIES OF ABOVE
APPLICATION TO GENERAL P...
VANCOUVER WINN...
MONTREAL QUE...

Canadian Nation...

Canadian National Railways,
Maclean's Magazine, June 15, 1920, p. 52

Preparing lunch,
Butterfly Lake, Muskoka

Girls' Technical School

Employees by Sex and Average Salaries and Wages Paid in Forty Leading Canadian Manufacturing Industries during 1927, with Average Number of Days Operated by Plants in each Industry for 1926 and 1927.

Industries	WAGES				
	Employees on Wages			Average Wage	Average number of days in operation
	Male	Female	Total	1926	1926
	No.	No.	No.	$	No.
Pulp and paper	28 889	813	29 702	1 302	281
Flour and grist mills	5 124	135	5 259	970	223
Slaughtering and meat-packing	7 492	711	8 203	1 101	288
Central electric stations	8 699	–	8 699	1 423	365
Sawmills	42 571	84	42 655	936	100
Automobiles	8 746	200	8 946	1 535	306
Butter and cheese	6 571	249	6 820	1 002	224
Rubber goods, including footwear	9 851	3 314	13 165	984	268
Electrical apparatus and supplies	9 926	2 865	12 791	1 061	291
Non-ferrous metal smelting	6 999	28	7 027	1 492	383
Cotton yarn and cloth	11 493	9 261	20 754	702	282
Railway rolling stock	19 996	45	20 041	1 329	277
Castings and forgings	16 516	352	16 868	1 138	294
Bread and other bakery products	11 786	1 782	13 568	1 069	299
Petroleum refining	3 311	26	3 337	1 479	309
Printing and publishing	7 892	1 389	9 281	1 365	299
Sugar refineries	2 253	112	2 365	1 157	245
Clothing, women's factory	3 757	10 137	13 894	880	283
Cigars and cigarettes	1 773	3 227	5 000	658	273
Hosiery, knit goods and gloves	4 874	11 285	16 159	728	283
Biscuits, confectionery and chewing gum	4 433	5 930	10 363	719	279
Breweries	3 763	44	3 807	1 186	293
Planing mills, sash and door factories	10 127	95	10 222	1 017	262
Boots and shoes, leather	8 562	5 530	14 092	883	287
Rolled products, pig iron, steel products, etc	6 864	3	6 867	1 382	288
Machinery	7 734	226	7 960	1 166	301
Sheet metal products	6 298	761	7 059	1 059	298
Clothing, men's factory	4 769	5 352	10 121	1 009	249
Agricultural implements	9 398	95	9 493	1 178	293
Printing and bookbinding	6 772	2 376	9 148	1 156	295
Furniture and upholstering	9 526	435	9 961	960	288
Leather tanneries	3 679	102	3 781	983	287
Fish-curing and packing	9 748	6 310	16 058	290	99
Acids, alkalies, salts and compressed gases	1 770	9	1 779	1 366	314
Furnishing goods, men's	1 104	7 072	8 176	646	290
Coffee and spices	648	420	1 068	877	299
Distilleries	916	227	1 143	1 109	268
Paints and varnishes	1 538	222	1 760	977	289
Hardware and tools	4 940	878	5 818	970	288
Brass and copper products	3 601	374	3 975	1 126	286
Total, forty leading industries	324 709	82 476	407 185	1 015	215
Grand Total, all industries	413 634	119 816	533 450	1 003	232

Many women who entered the work force during World War I resisted social pressures to quit their jobs when the war ended, and continued working during the 1920s.

14

Canada Year Book

LEAD A DOUBLE LIFE"

Nellie McClung was a tireless fighter for women's rights in Canada. After her election to the Manitoba legislature in 1921, she began to improve conditions for the rights of women. Nellie McClung and a group known as the "Alberta Five" won for women the right to be appointed to the Canadian Senate.

LEGAL STATUS OF WOMEN IN CANADA, 1925

"On the presentation of a request by the National Council of Women, which links together a very large number of women's organizations in the cities and towns of Canada, the Dominion Government recently agreed to publish a pamphlet designed to give briefly the main sections of the federal and provincial statutes which deal with the relations of women in the family, in industry, in the municipality, and in the state. As the legislation involved is of a social character and various phases of it have been the subject of discussion and resolutions by labour organizations, it was decided that publication should be made under the authority of the Minister of Labour.

"The Department of Labour has, therefore, issued a pamphlet containing extracts from the Dominion and provincial laws relating to naturalization, franchise, eligibility of women for municipal, provincial or federal election and for service as magistrates or jurors, marriage, divorce, sexual offences, married women's earnings and property, dower, devolution of estates, insurance, mothers' pensions, maternity benefits, deserted wives and children, legitimation of children born out of wedlock, support of children of unmarried parents, adoption of children, hours of labour and minimum wages for employed women, workmen's compensation, and other minor subjects.

"Laws enabling the establishment of minimum rates of wages for the employment of women have been passed in all the provinces but New Brunswick and Prince Edward Island. The Quebec statute, however, is not in force and no regulations have been issued in Nova Scotia. Compensation to the dependents of a man or woman injured in the course of employment is payable in all the provinces but Prince Edward Island."

Labour Gazette 1925

Women Win Vote
May 24, 1918

FINE WORK BY WOMEN'S INSTITUTES

Large Attendance at Tenth Annual Convention Now In Session

Various Institutes of Province Are "Carrying On" In Excellent Manner

Halifax Herald, June 21, 1923

The First Great Political Convention for Women

Having regard to the evolution now going on in the minds of our Canadian women in connection with not only party politics, but the whole matter of political expression, it may be stated that two main features emerged very clearly from the first national convention of Liberal women which was held in Ottawa in the middle of April last, and that these two features are probably as applicable to Conservative as to Liberal women.

The first is, that it was made abundantly clear throughout all the proceedings that our women are, at last, attaining some measure of political consciousness, with a corresponding desire to use their political power as adequately as possible.

The second is that experience in practical politics has shown in the past ten years in all the provinces of Canada, as it has shown in all parts of the United States, that this political consciousness can best express itself and most effectively operate in separate organizations of women within the party folds, even though the ultimate ideal of women and men working side by side in the political arena, be strongly held.

This conference, the first of its kind, undoubtedly marks a new era in so far as Canadian women in politics are concerned. It has been in the air a long time, was indeed long overdue, and will undoubtedly be followed by some such gathering of the women of the Conservative party to effect a similar national organization.

The Chatelaine, June, 1928

Women's organizations grew rapidly during the 1920s, there were at least 60 country-wide organizations by 1929. Of these, the largest was the Women's Institute: by 1922 there were 1 000 chapters in Ontario. Their objective was "the dissemination of knowledge relating to domestic economy, with special attention to home and sanitation; a better understanding of foods, and a more scientific care and training of children to raise the general standing of health and morals of our people."

"That's just what I mean, every woman should lead a double life.... The married woman answers to her father and mother, her husband's father and mother.... She answers the grocer, the butcher and the public ownership collectors, if the bills are not paid. She answers the doctor if she deviates from the diet he has laid down for the baby. She answers her husband pleasantly when he comes in the house.

"Every woman should have as distinctly dual a life interest as has the average man. Man has his home life and his business life, and if he is wise he keeps them widely separated.

"Woman, too, should have a double life."

by Margaret Fea, *The Chatelaine*, Apr. 1928.

15

A CHILD GROWING UP...

Children walking to school in High Park, Toronto, 1929

18-147. Toy Drum with a good tone, sheepskin and fibre heads, 8 inches in diameter, brightly lithographed with Canadian emblem. Complete with two drum sticks. Price.................**49c**

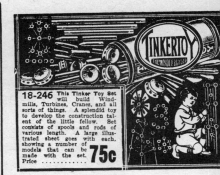

18-246 This Tinker Toy Set will build Windmills, Turbines, Cranes, and all sorts of things. A splendid toy to develop the construction talent of the little fellow. Set consists of spools and rods of various length. A large illustrated sheet goes with each, showing a number of models that can be made with the set. Price **75c**

18-117. I'm a Walker. A brightly lithographed cardboard doll, 12-ins. long, supplied with 12-in. wood handle. Can really walk. A splendid push toy. Price. **25c**

GIRLS

Height 8¾-in.

19-209. Toy Dresser in which to keep doll's clothes. Made of wood, well made and finished, 4 drawers and oblong mirror, size 5 x 3, height to top of mirror 8¾ ins. Price................**85c**

SCHOOL DAYS

Elementary school classroom

STATISTICAL OUTLINE OF CANADIAN EDUCATION

EDUCATION	1911	1916	1921	1924	1925	1926	1927
Enrolment	1 356 879	1 622 351	1 869 643	2 013 158	2 034 080	2 063 498	2 076 284
Average daily attendance	870 801	1 140 793	1 335 454	1 506 698	1 524 665	1 547 992	1 563 212
Number of teachers	40 516	50 307	56 607	62 302	62 394	63 840	66 004
Total Public Expenditure	$37 971 374	$57 362 734	$112 976 543	$119 484 033	$121 034 234	$122 701 259	$125 876 375

Canada Year Book, 1929

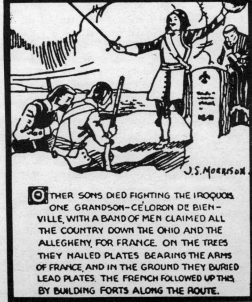

OTHER SONS DIED FIGHTING THE IROQUOIS. ONE GRANDSON—CÉLORON DE BIENVILLE, WITH A BAND OF MEN CLAIMED ALL THE COUNTRY DOWN THE OHIO AND THE ALLEGHENY, FOR FRANCE. ON THE TREES THEY NAILED PLATES BEARING THE ARMS OF FRANCE, AND IN THE GROUND THEY BURIED LEAD PLATES. THE FRENCH FOLLOWED UP THIS BY BUILDING FORTS ALONG THE ROUTE.

sketch by J. S. Morrison
M. M. Stone, *This Canada of Ours,* p. 107

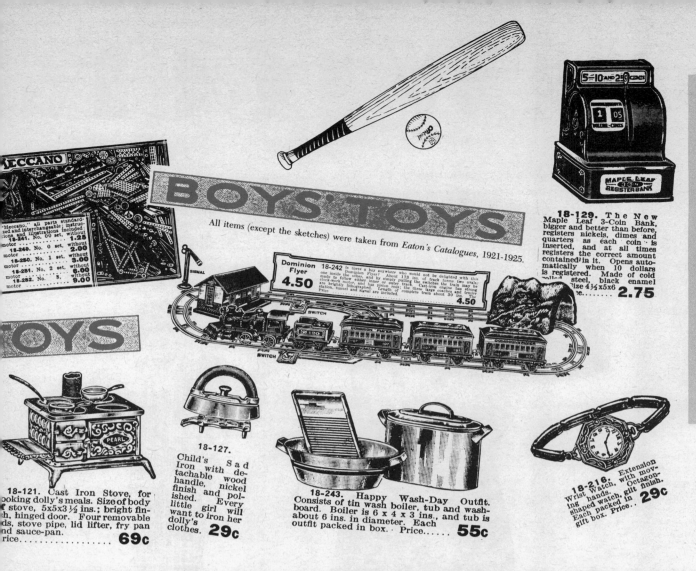

BOYS' TOYS

All items (except the sketches) were taken from *Eaton's Catalogues, 1921-1925.*

MECCANO, "all parts standardized and interchangeable, instructions and illustrations included
18-261. No. 00 set, without motor 1.25
18-249. No. 0 set, without motor 2.00
18-250. No. 1 set, without motor 3.00
18-251. No. 2 set, without motor 6.00
18-252. No. 3. without motor 9.00

18-242. Is there a boy anywhere who would not be delighted with this one inside the **Dominion Flyer**? About 173 ins. of track forms two ovals...
Dominion Flyer 4.50
4.50

18-129. The New Maple Leaf 3-Coin Bank, bigger and better than before, registers nickels, dimes and quarters as each coin is inserted, and at all times registers the correct amount contained in it. Opens automatically when 10 dollars is registered. Made of cold steel, black enamel ... Size 4½ x5x6 ... 2.75

18-121. Cast Iron Stove, for cooking dolly's meals. Size of body of stove, 5x5x3½ ins.; bright finish, hinged door. Four removable lids, stove pipe, lid lifter, fry pan and sauce-pan. Price 69c

18-127. Child's Sad Iron with detachable wood handle, nickel finish and polished. Every little girl will want to iron her dolly's clothes. 29c

18-243. Happy Wash-Day Outfit. Consists of tin wash boiler, tub and washboard. Boiler is 6 x 4 x 3 ins., and tub is about 6 ins. in diameter. Each outfit packed in box. Price 55c

18-216. Extension Wrist Watch, with moving hands. Octagon-shaped watch, gilt finish. Each packed in gift box. Price .. 29c

HOW MY FATHER DISCIPLINED ME

"Whenever I misbehaved, my parents gave me a stern look. If that didn't work, my father took off his belt and gave me a licking on the rear end. My loud yells were usually sufficient warning to my brother and sister not to follow my actions. If there was company at our home and I misbehaved, mother or father gave me that same stern look which meant I would get spanked later. It was a rule that we were never scolded or spanked in front of company. But there were also many times my parents took time to talk with me if I did something wrong."

HISTORY TEST

1. Give an account of the parts played in Canadian history by any three of the following:—
(a) Sir John A. Macdonald.
(b) Hon. George Brown.
(c) Sir Wilfrid Laurier.
(d) Lord Durham.
(e) Sir George Etienne Cartier.
(f) Sir Isaac Brock.

2. (a) Give the chief provisions of the British North America Act.
(b) State the circumstances under which British Columbia and Manitoba became provinces of Canada.

OR

(a) Give the name by which the official is known who is at the head of each of the following: a township council, a county council, a town (or city) council.
(b) By whom are the members of the Senate appointed?
(c) Name two matters over which the Dominion Government has control and two matters over which the Provincial Legislature has control. *Examination Papers, Ontario Ministry of Education*

ENGLISH GRAMMAR TEST

1. Write the following sentences, selecting from the brackets the proper word in each case; give reasons for your choice:—
(a) I saw the man (who, whom) you met last evening.
(b) (Was, Were) either of the men here?
(c) He has (less, fewer) friends each year.
(d) The number of automobile accidents (is, are) very large.
(e) He walks very (slow, slowly). *Examination Papers, Ontario Ministry of Education*

ARITHMETIC TEST

1. For $1 500 a dealer bought a farmer's crop of 380 barrels of apples. To pick and pack the apples the dealer paid 8 men for 5 days at $3.50 per day each. He also paid 75 cents for each barrel and $130 for freight and cartage. At what price per barrel must he sell the apples to make a clear gain of $225?

2. A man built a house valued at $5 000. He insured it for one year for 75% of its value at 60 cents per hundred dollars. He paid taxes at 30 mills on the dollar on 80% of its value. How much did he pay for both insurance and taxes? *Examination Papers, Ontario Ministry of Education*

Boys' Technical School

A NEW LOOK

TEDDY
49c

TEDDY wears overalls of khaki, or navy, trimmed on the knees and pockets with cardinal. They're cool and airy, and easy to wash. Sizes 2 to 6 years. P r i c e , 49c.— Third Floor, James St.

A—All-wool cardigans, consistently match their socks—or vice versa. In plain heather-toned mixtures, checks, and colorful fancy patterns, V-neck style, with two pockets. Sizes 36 to 44, each $10.50. Matching hose, $5.00 a pair.—Main Floor, Queen Street

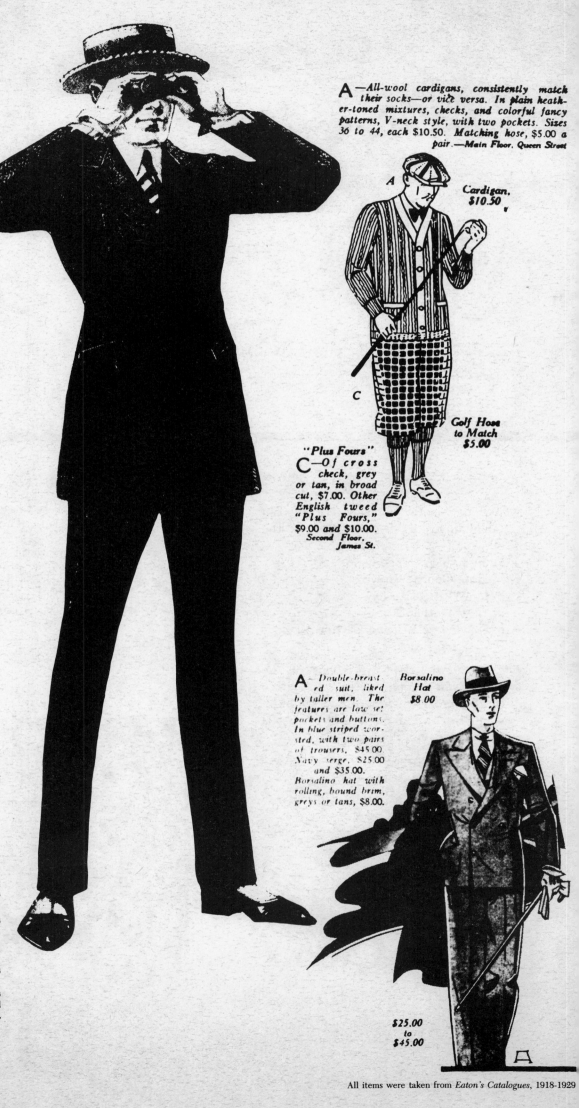

A

Cardigan,
$10.50

C

Golf Hose
to Match
$5.00

They Will Like the Comfort Of These Summer Clothes

JACK is now twelve years old, and wears long khaki trousers and outing shirt of heavy twill cotton. The shirts are on the Main Floor, Queen St. Sizes 12 to 14½. Price, $1.10. The trousers on the Second Floor. Sizes 6 to 10 years, $1.25 pair. Sizes 11 to 18 years, $1.50.

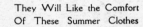

MARIE
Skirt
$1.98
Bloomers
$1.98

JACK
Shirt, $1.25.
Trousers, $1.45.

MARIE'S mother dresses her in khaki cotton middy and bloomers, about the camp or garden. The bloomers are very full, pleated on a waist band. Both are in sizes 6 to 14. Priced at $1.98 each for middy and bloomers.—Fourth Floor, Centre.

"Plus Fours"
C—Of cross check, grey or tan, in broad cut, $7.00. Other English tweed "Plus Fours," $9.00 and $10.00. Second Floor, James St.

Dark Grey Tweed In Three-in-One Style

SIZES:
34 in. chest with 30 in. waist only
35 in. chest with 31 in. waist only
36 in. chest with 32 in. waist only
37 in. chest with 33 in. waist only
38 in. chest with 34 in. waist only
39 in. chest with 35 in. waist only
Choice of leg lengths 29 to 33 ins.

44-532 This splendid suit, made of a good wearing dark grey cotton and wool tweed, is tailored in the three-in-one style. Can be worn as belter; with belt removed as a waistline model, or with strap waistline removed as a plain two-button single-breasted coat. High-peaked roll lapels with slightly slanting welt pockets; five-button vest; cuff bottom trousers with five pockets and belt loops. Well tailored throughout. State correct size, height and weight when ordering.

Price, delivered

33.75

A—Double-breast ed suit, liked by taller men. The features are low set pockets and buttons. In blue striped worsted, with two pairs of trousers, $45.00. Navy serge, $25.00 and $35.00. Borsalino hat with rolling, bound brim, greys or tans, $8.00.

Borsalino
Hat
$8.00

$25.00
to
$45.00

FOR CANADIANS

Mr. and Mrs. Snell on their wedding day,
1928, Dashwood, Ontario

Stylish and Inexpensive

(See Table of Sizes to Left).
Color Navy with White only.

84-291 Navy All-Wool Serge with a white hairline stripe is the smart, service-giving fabric that fashions this straight-line model for misses. Insets of the material with the stripes running across extend from beneath pointed button-trimmed flaps on pockets. Long set-in sleeves have turn-back cuffs while jaunty self tie and girdle make a swagger finish. "EATON-MADE." Finished with deep basted hem. Price.... **7.50**

7.50

A—A charming version of the new three-piece jacket frock, developed in pitch pine green wool jersey, with a matching sleeveless blouse of crepe-de-Chine. The jacket exploits horizontal tucks and a fabric flower, while narrow side pleats give skirt fulness. Also in light tan with rose beige, navy with sand or grey, queen blue or almond green, $19.50.

$19.50

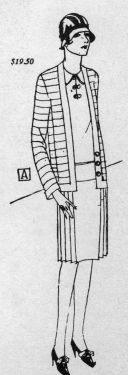

Misses' New Hat

Choice of Wood (light) Brown, Sand, Henna, Saxe Blue, Purple Almond Green or Black.

51-217 **3.95**
Misses' stylish Hat of Velvet, combined with Fine Art Silk. Pretty embroidered trimming in harmonizing colors. Head-size about 22½ ins.

5.95 Misses' Fashionable Skirt of All-Wool Flannel

Color Cream only.

Waistbands 24, 25, 26, 27, 28 ins. Choice of front lengths 30, 32, 34 ins.

84-512 All-wool Flannel is a favorite Cream-colored skirt, of which this is such a handsome version. Its material is of an excellent quality having a rich, smooth finish, while the inset pockets are stressed by fine silk embroidery stitching. On this model that is made in our own workrooms, slight fulness is controlled by gathers beneath button-trimmed belt. Price.... **5.95**

A New Look...

Silk Crepe-de-Chine Model

Bust sizes 34, 36, 38, 40, 42, 44, 46.
Choice of Black, Grey or Sand.

78-546 Tucks are in high favor as trimmings this season and groups of pin tucks separated by a little space from groups of wider ones are arranged, as illustrated, on front of this appealing Overblouse. The material is Silk Crepe-de-Chine and it is also used to cover buttons and form loops that effect closing at neck. Like so many of the new models it has puff sleeves and the cuffs fasten with hook and eye. Doublefold of the Crepe-de-Chine composes nicely-fitting collar and hipband that buttons at side. State size and color desired when ordering. Price.... **5.95**

5.95

Misses' Bodice Skirt of Serge **5.95**

Color Navy only.

Skirt lengths, 30, 32, 34 ins.

84-514 The new and practical Bodice Skirt is here introduced, this one being developed for misses with pleated skirt section of fine, soft All-wool Serge attached to a white silk bodice. The narrow box pleats make this a particularly happy example of this slipover style which is the correct accompaniment for an overblouse or the modish Jacquette. "EATON-MADE." Price.. **5.95**

When Ordering by Mail

THE WORKER

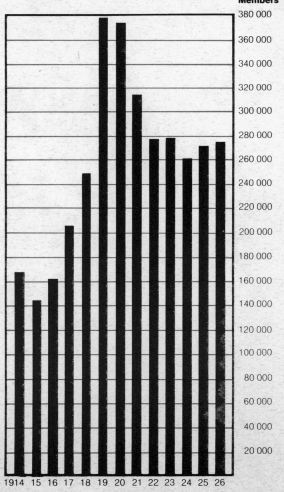

THE SAME OLD STORY

The [London] Herald, Aug. 17, 1921

LAW AND ORDER TO BE ENFORCED

Premier Makes Statement Regarding Labor Situation In Canada.

CO-OPERATION IS NEEDED

Hopes For Every Facility For Discussion With Employers.

CANNOT ENACT 8-HOUR DAY.
OTTAWA, May 27.—In the House this afternoon W. D. Euler asked if the Government proposed to enact legislation to make an eight-hour day compulsory, to which Hon. Mr. MacLean replied that it was not within the legislative jurisdiction of Canada to enact an eight-hour day law.

Special to The Free Press.
OTTAWA, May 27. — Sir Robert Borden made a statement in the House

London Free Press, May 28, 1919

A WORKINGMAN'S STORY

"I served with Canada's armed forces in the Great War and looked forward to returning to my family and work in 1919. But I was not the only one with this idea, there were thousands of returning veterans looking for jobs that didn't exist. Prices were high and it was difficult to provide for my family's needs. I eventually did find work in a Hamilton factory but there were lots of men who were not so lucky."

EMPLOYEES WORKING A SPECIFIED NUMBER OF HOURS PER DAY, JUNE, 1919.

Hours	Men	Women	Total	Percentage
4	26	.....	26	.....
5	119	146	265	.....
5.5	.....	2	2	.....
6	164	460	624	.....
6.5	89	190	279	.....
7	3 908	4 180	8 088	1.4
7.5	4 300	3 512	7 818	1.4
8*	222 910	43 356	266 236	43.4
8.5	22 527	10 740	33 267	5.4
9	123 987	28 742	152 729	24.9
9.5	7 549	2 358	9 907	1.6
10	106 450	14 277	120 727	19.7
10.5	1 474	184	1 658	.2
11	3 654	71	3 725	.6
11.5	56	.....	56	.....
12	5 393	37	5 430	.8
12.5	145	.....	145	.....
13	966	26	992	.....
14	266	3	269	.....
15	5	.....	5	.....
17	150	.....	150	.....
	504 134	108 254	612 398	.....

*Including 100 000 steam railway employees, as a proportionate number.
Labour Gazette 1920

WAGES AND HOURS, 1920		
Bricklayer	$1.00 per h	44 h w
Carpenter	.90	44
Electrician	.875	44
Painter	.75	44
Plumber	.90	14
Metal Worker	.65-.80	48
Builder's Labourer	.55-.65	44
Factory Labourer	.40	50

Canadian Wage Rates and Hours of Labour, 1901-1930.

The chief causes of unrest may be enumerated as follows:
1. Unemployment and the fear of unemployment.
2. High cost of living in relation to wages and the desire of the worker for a larger share of the product of his labour.
3. Desire for shorter hours of labour.
4. Denial of the right to organize and refusal to recognize Unions.
5. Denial of collective bargaining.
6. Lack of confidence in constituted government.
7. Insufficient and poor housing.
8. Restrictions upon the freedom of speech and press.
9. Ostentatious display of wealth.
10. Lack of equal educational opportunities. *Labour Gazette 1919*

TRADE UNIONISM IN CANADA

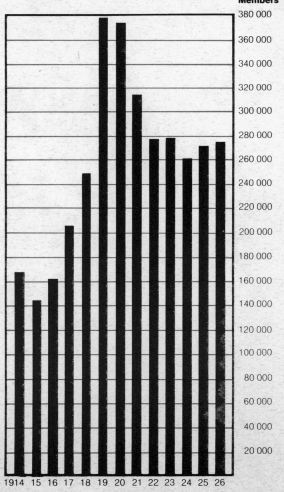

Members — 380 000, 360 000, 340 000, 320 000, 300 000, 280 000, 260 000, 240 000, 220 000, 200 000, 180 000, 160 000, 140 000, 120 000, 100 000, 80 000, 60 000, 40 000, 20 000

1914 15 16 17 18 19 20 21 22 23 24 25 26

Labour Organizations in Canada, 1924-26

Boys as young as nine years of age worked in the British Columbia mines as mule boys before 1920. Child labour became illegal during the 1920s.

WINNIPEG GENERAL STRIKE, 1919

WINNIPEG GENERAL STRIKE, 1919

WINNIPEG GENERAL STRIKE

- May 15, 1919 – Trade and Labour Councils call a general strike
- 25 000 of Winnipeg's work force participate
- May 19 – bread and milk deliveries resume
- May 24 – Federal government intervenes by ordering postal employees to return to work
- unemployed war veterans stage parades for and against the strike
- June 9 – City Council dismisses Winnipeg Police Force
- June 16-17 – eight strike leaders arrested
- June 21 – "Bloody Saturday"
- June 25 – Trades and Labour Council ends strike

STRIKES AND LOCKOUTS

Those who lost
Those who won
Those who compromised
Indefinite

People

140 000
130 000
120 000
110 000
100 000
90 000
80 000
70 000
60 000
50 000
40 000
30 000
20 000
10 000

1917 18 19 20 21 22 23 24

FRED TIPPING, A PROMINENT LEADER OF THE WINNIPEG GENERAL STRIKE WAS INTERVIEWED IN 1973.

"It was the demand on the part of the workers for the right of collective bargaining. The government was on record as favouring it, trade unions were legal organizations. There were already some craft unions, but for the most part business refused to recognize the existence of unions. . . . Judged by conditions of today it is certainly remarkable that there was so little violence. There was no looting or stealing. Again and again the strike committee repeated the maxim and posted it all over the place – DO NOTHING. . . . While it is true that labour did not gain its immediate objective, it gained for the trade union movement a recognition. All the men who were imprisoned, or others active in the strike, received public recognition."

Canadian Dimension, May, 1973

Mob Attacked Mounted Police Who Were Forced to Fire—Riot Act Read

Mike Sokolowski, a Registered Alien Shot Through Heart and Instantly Killed, Presumably While Stooping to Pick Up Missile—Thirty of Injured, Including Several Members of R.N.W.M.P., Taken to Hospital, But Ten Were Sent Home After Minor Wounds Had Been Treated—Believed All of Injured Will Recover—Police Did Not Open Fire Until Several Minutes After Riot Act Was Read, and In Majority of Cases Fired Into Pavement Or Into Air—Police Fired On From Roofs and Windows—Military Called Out to Help Suppress Riot *Winnipeg Free Press, June 23, 1919*

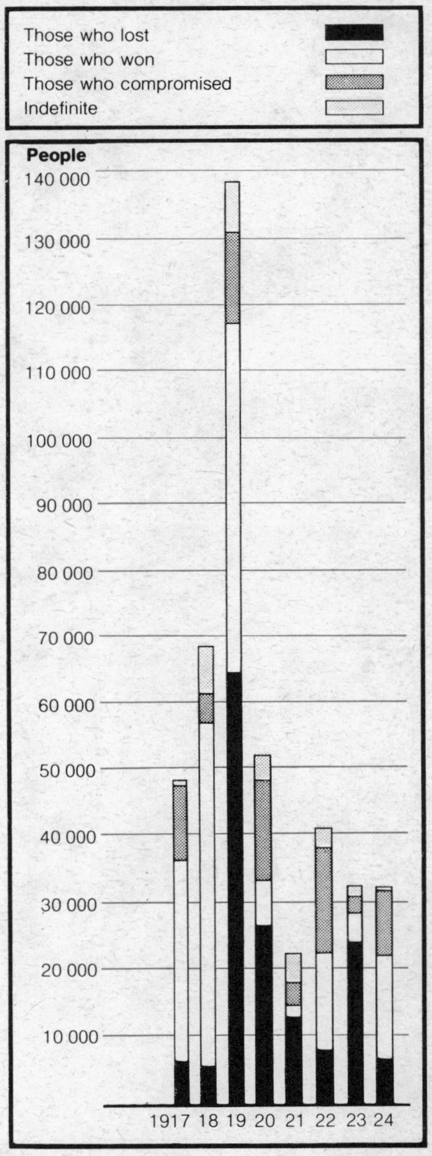

...OLLEY OVER HEADS OF ...CROWD, FIRST SHOTS IN ...STEEL STRIKE AT SYDNEY

Nights of Excitement at Coke Ovens District of Steel Plant—Troops Fired Over Heads of Strikers on Saturday Night, And Began to Mount Machine Gun—Last Night Saw Charges by Mounted Provincial Police, Local Police Sorties And Armed Troops in Warlike Attitude—Several Men Received Injuries—Two Are Under Arrest.

Halifax Herald, July 2, 1923

GENERAL STRIKE CALLED FOR NOON TODAY: MINERS SUPPORT SCOTIA TIE-UP

Mass Meeting at Glace Bay Decides Upon Complete Walkout in Cape Breton Unless Men Are Reinstated —Some Seven Thousand Would be Affected—Mines On North Side of Sydney Harbor Are Idle; And Pitmen of South Side Take Sympathetic Stand.

Halifax Herald, June 15, 1923

1923 CAPE BRETON COAL STRIKE,

The Canadian army camped outside of Sydney, Nova Scotia steel plant, 1923.

Balloon bursting race at a Toronto Transit Commission Picnic, July, 1926

Manitoba Free Press, Aug. 6, 1927.

AFTER WORK: ENTERTAINMENT AND CULTURE

The silver and silent [movie] screen arrived across Canada in the cities, and towns of over 5 000 people. Canadians enjoyed a wide range of talent in films featuring such stars as Charlie Chaplin, Douglas Fairbanks Jr., Toronto-born Mary Pickford and Clara Bow, the "It" Girl. The 451 theatres of Canada presented a mixture of stage, vaudeville and motion picture entertainment throughout the 1920s. The first two rapidly disappeared when the "talkies" arrived in 1928.

Mary Pickford plays Little Annie Rooney.

DANCES OF THE 1920s	
Shimmy	Waltz
Black Bottom	Fox-Trot
Bunny Hop	Tango
Charleston	Turkey Trot
Butterfly	Cheek to Cheek
Strut	

AS COOL AS THE BEACHES

Metropolitan

TODAY:
"METROPOLIS"

STARTING TOMORROW:

Tender Hour

BILLIE DOVE BEN LYON

REGULAR PRICES

Manitoba Free Press. Aug. 19, 1927

Ontario Agricultural College Orchestra, Guelph, Ontario, 1922-23

1920s HIT PARADE
1. Ain't We Got Fun
2. Sweet Georgia Brown
3. Birth of the Blues
4. Bye Bye Blackbird
5. When the Red, Red Robin Comes Bob, Bob Bobbin' Along.
6. It Ain't Gonna Rain No More.
7. I'm Looking over a Four Leaf Clover
8. Happy Days Are Here Again
9. Tea for Two
10. Look For the Silver Lining
11. Yes, We Have No Bananas
12. Sunny Side up
13. This Is My Lucky Day
14. Barney Google
15. Let's Do It, Let's Fall In Love

AUG 6TH 1927

A couple dancing the Charleston

London Free Press. Oct. 18, 1929

Sleighing, snowshoeing, and skiing were all popular winter sports at Toronto's High Park.

A great source of family fun was the company picnic. Here the line-up waits for free ice-cream, summer of '29

Country church scene

The church in rural and small-town Canada was the centre of social life for young and old alike. If a congregation was big enough to support its own clergyman, religious services were often held twice on Sunday.

During the week, according to the seasons, there were other church-centred activities such as strawberry socials and free harvest suppers.

In the winter months, a young people's group often put on a play and a box lunch social. The play was rehearsed in homes on cold winter evenings; a box lunch was put together and decorated by each girl, to be bid upon by her favorite young man. Occasionally some smart alec might bid against her steady beau, forcing the price of the box lunch up to $7 or $8. In this way the group raised money for items such as gramophones and phonograph records.

THE GROUP OF SEVEN

J. E. H. MacDonald   Frank Johnston   Franklin Carmichael
A. Y. Jackson   Arthur Lismer   Fred Varley   Lawren Harris

In 1920 a group of painters mostly from Ontario and Quebec decided to form "a friendly alliance for defence" against negative responses to their work from art critics, other artists and the Canadian public. Named the Group of Seven, they had worked closely with Tom Thomson (who drowned in a mysterious accident on Canoe Lake in Algonquin Park in 1917) and they inspired others such as Emily Carr of Victoria, B.C.

Determined to paint Canada in a new and distinctive manner, the Group despite their fears met with critical acclaim and much public acceptance. In fact, their very success in encouraging Canadians to appreciate the beauty of Canada's landscapes and Canadian artistic interpretation made it rather difficult for other artists of the time to develop a diversity of styles and subjects.

Band Stand at Sunnyside Beach, Toronto, June 18, 1924

The 1928 Olympic 400 metre team: Jane Bell, Myrtle Cook, Ethel Smith, and Bobbie Rosenfeld

1928 Olympics at Amsterdam

The Canadian team won 15 medals in an outstanding Olympic performance. The six Canadian women won more points, as a team, than any other nation.

The Edmonton Grads

Edmonton Grads' Record

- won 502, lost 20
- Grads: 1 863 points; opponents: 297 points
- won 4 Olympic victories at Amsterdam, Paris, Berlin, and Los Angeles
- Grads won 7 out of 9 against mens' teams.

They were called "the greatest team that ever stepped out on a basketball floor".

Ada MacKenzie won the Canadian Women's Open in 1919, and the Ontario Open in 1922. In all, she won the Ontario Open eleven times.

Ethel Catherwood was a popular member of the Olympic team, and was nicknamed "The Saskatoon Lily". Her great achievement was setting a new Olympic world record in the high jump (160.02 cm).

1919— Canada had about 100 golf courses

1925— Canada had 292 golf courses

Sandy Sommerville was Canada's outstanding amateur golfer in the 1920s.

The schooner *Bluenose* won a number of international sailing events. Captain Angus Walters and his racing crew of 32 men were one of the most successful teams in sailboat racing history.

Bill Cook, Frank Boucher, and Bun Cook, all played for the New York Rangers in the season of 1926-27.

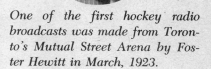

One of the first hockey radio broadcasts was made from Toronto's Mutual Street Arena by Foster Hewitt in March, 1923.

GREY CUP

The Grey Cup was awarded for the "Rugby Football Championship" of Canada. In 1921, teams from Western Canada were permitted to challenge for the Grey Cup for the first time, making the finals truly national in scope. That year the Toronto Argos defeated Edmonton 23-0.

Football game at C.N.E. grounds, 1926

Rugby Records

The standings of the clubs in various rugby unions and groups, including games played on Saturday, are:

Senior Intercollegiate	P	W	L	F	A	Pts
Queen's	4	4	0	72	7	8
Toronto	4	3	1	52	17	6
McGill	4	1	3	12	57	2
Western Ont.	4	0	4	13	68	0

Games next Saturday—Toronto at McGill, Western Ontario at Queen's

Senior Interprovincial	P	W	L	F	A	Pts
Hamilton	4	3	1	74	16	6
Montreal	4	3	1	15	23	6
Argonauts	4	2	2	33	13	4
Ottawa	4	0	3	8	80	0

Games next Saturday—Montreal at Argonauts, Hamilton at Ottawa

Senior O.R.F.F. Group No. 1	P	W	L	F	A	Pts
Balmy Beach	4	4	0	48	13	8
Kitchener	5	3	2	57	30	6
St. Michael's	4	2	2	37	48	4
Camp Borden	5	0	5	11	62	0

Games next Saturday—Kitchener at Camp Borden, Balmy Beach at St. Michael's

Group No. 2	P	W	L	F	A	Pts
Sarnia	4	4	0	63	11	8
Windsor	6	2	2	28	41	4
Hamilton	4	2	2	24	40	4
Varsity	4	0	4	27	50	0

Games next Saturday—Sarnia at Hamilton, Windsor at Varsity

Percy Williams won a gold medal in the 100 metres (10.8 s).

A curling match

PROHIBITION ACT OF BRITISH COLUMBIA
May 31, 1916

"No person shall within the province, by himself or agent ... expose or keep for sale ... or offer to sell or barter or in consideration of the purchase or transfer of any property or thing or for any other consideration ... give to any other person any liquor." [Section 10]

EXCEPTIONS

(a) When sold for a mechanical or scientific purpose

(b) When sold for medicinal purposes – doctors, dentists, veterinaries

(c) When sold for sacramental purposes

(d) When sold by government-appointed vendors

(e) When sold by a brewer, distiller, or any other person licensed by the Government of Canada for the manufacture and keeping of spirituous, fermented, or other liquors

(f) When sold by a person who has a separate warehouse for the sole purpose of selling or exporting liquor for export from the province

(g) When owned by a private person within a private dwelling house

CONTROLS

(a) Every brewer and distiller or other person licensed by the Government of Canada, and every liquor exporter must keep records of sale showing the date of purchase, the purchaser, and the carrier.

(b) Government-appointed vendors shall keep a record of the purchaser, affidavits of use, prescriptions, and written requests.

PENALTIES

(a) Every person contravening Section 10 upon conviction is liable to imprisonment, with hard labour, for a term not less than six months, and not more than twelve months for the first offence.

(b) If the offender be a corporation, it shall be liable to a penalty of one thousand dollars.

Provincial Archives of British Columbia

PROHIBITION: A STATE OF CONFUSION

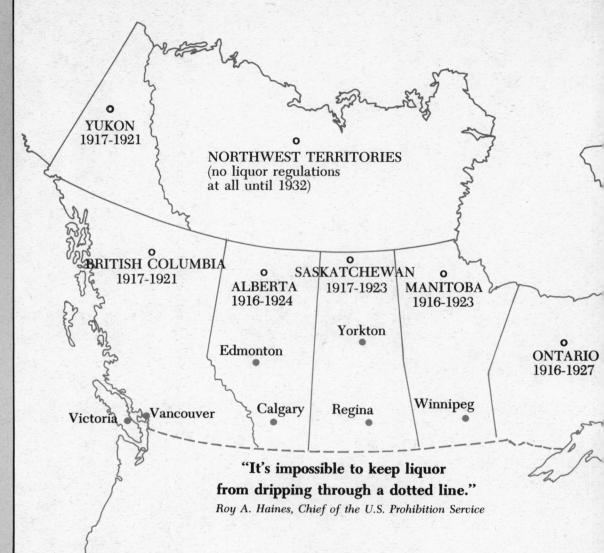

YUKON
1917-1921

NORTHWEST TERRITORIES
(no liquor regulations
at all until 1932)

BRITISH COLUMBIA
1917-1921

ALBERTA
1916-1924

SASKATCHEWAN
1917-1923

MANITOBA
1916-1923

Yorkton

Edmonton

ONTARIO
1916-1927

Victoria · Vancouver   Calgary   Regina   Winnipeg

"It's impossible to keep liquor from dripping through a dotted line."
Roy A. Haines, Chief of the U.S. Prohibition Service

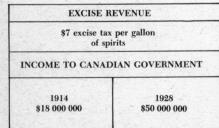

EXCISE REVENUE	
$7 excise tax per gallon of spirits	
INCOME TO CANADIAN GOVERNMENT	
1914 $18 000 000	1928 $50 000 000

J. C. Furnas, *Great Times: An Informal Social History of the United States*, p. 347

ROYAL COMMISSION INVESTIGATING CUSTOMS AND EXCISE, 1926

"Virtually every distillery, brewery and liquor exporter found it expedient to either burn or lose their company's doctored ledgers. The government sued 30 of them but collected only a piddling $3 000 000 in back taxes"

"When Canada Ran the Rum" by Frank Rasky, *The Canadian* Magazine, Nov. 1, 1969

The Elk Lake blind pig was raided and 160 kegs were destroyed.

ALBERTA		
	1915	1920
BREWERIES	7	5
ACTUAL SALES (Including bootlegging activity)	$14 000 000	$5 000 000

R. Allen, *The Social Passion: Religion and Social Reform in Canada*, p. 270

Key
- ○ Periods of Prohibition
- ● Centres with warehouses where liquor was exported to the U.S.

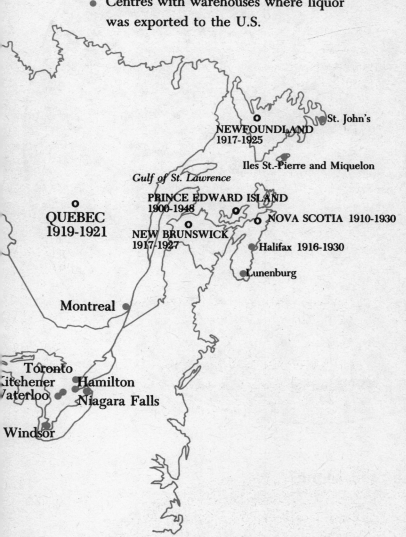

ST. JOHN'S
NEWFOUNDLAND 1917-1925
Iles St.-Pierre and Miquelon
Gulf of St. Lawrence
PRINCE EDWARD ISLAND 1900-1948
QUEBEC 1919-1921
NOVA SCOTIA 1910-1930
NEW BRUNSWICK 1917-1927
Halifax 1916-1930
Lunenburg
Montreal
Toronto
Kitchener
Waterloo
Hamilton
Niagara Falls
Windsor

ONTARIO
6 distilleries and 29 breweries operated almost undisturbed throughout the prohibition era.

G. A. Hallowell, *Prohibition in Ontario 1919-1923*, p. 117.

ANTI-PROHIBITION REMEDIES		
Should B.C. go dry, don't forget that your druggist can supply you with big doses of alcohol in the following patent medicines:		
Hamlin's Wizard Oil	65%	alcohol
Hall's Great Discovery	43%	alcohol
Hamlin's Remedy	22%	alcohol
Paine's Celery Compound	20%	alcohol
Wine of Cardin	20%	alcohol
Peruna	18%	alcohol
Lydia E. Pinkham's Vegetable Compound	18%	alcohol
Rexall's Rheumatic Remedy	18%	alcohol
Electric Brand Bitters	18%	alcohol
Buchu Juniper Compound	16%	alcohol
Carter's Physical Extract	22%	alcohol
Hooker's Wigwam Tonic	20.7%	alcohol
Liebig Company's Coca Beef Tonic	23.2%	alcohol
Burdock Blood Bitters	25%	alcohol
Hop Bitters	12%	alcohol

Provincial Archives of British Columbia

GOVERNMENT CONTROL IS GOING TO WIN VOTE FOR IT

---because:

Prohibition is compulsion, and can never be enforced because public opinion is NOT behind it.

It is impossible to make men temperate by legislation. This can only be accomplished by force of example and education.

Direct taxation cannot be avoided if the Government Control Act is not endorsed. Direct taxation to balance the Government Budget would cost each head of a family from $20.00 up to $30.00 per year.

Vote Government Control to put the three million of dollars made by the bootleggers annually into the Public Treasury for public services.

Dominion Bureau of Statistics prove that Government Control has decreased the consumption of alcoholic liquors in Canada by 37%.

Old Age Pensions and Mothers' Allowances can be made possible if Government Control is endorsed.

Tourist traffic will be greatly increased if Nova Scotia adopts Government Control of liquor.

Vote Government Control to protect our young people from secret drinking now prevalent under the Nova Scotia Temperance Act.

Remember Joseph Howe condemned a prohibitory law as impossible of enforcement in 1854. His judgment has been vindicated.

The medical profession condemn prohibition. Cases of acute and chronic alcoholism have increased tremendously at the Victoria General Hospital, Halifax, under the N.S.T.A.

Labor has always been opposed to prohibition and will support Government Control almost 100 percent.

Who Is Entitled To Vote?

Any person may vote in the district in which they reside even if their name is not on the list, upon presenting themselves at the poll and taking an oath to the effect that he or she is a British subject, is 21 years of age, and has resided in the province of Nova Scotia for the last twelve months and being vouched for by a duly qualified voter whose name does appear on the list.

Railway employees, fishermen, sailors, and commercial travellers may vote anywhere in the Province upon subscribing the oath of qualification as above set forth.

Take This Sample Ballot to the Poll With You to Assist You in Marking Your Ballot Correctly.

MARK YOUR BALLOT LIKE THIS

	YES	NO
1. Are you in favor of continuing the Nova Scotia Temperance Act?		X
2. Are you in favor of the sale of alcoholic Liquors under a Government Control Act?	X	

DO NOT WRITE YES or NO MARK X

TEMPERANCE REFORM ASSOCIATION

Halifax Herald, October 30, 1929

REVENUE AND CONSUMPTION
The Canadian revenue collected from beer and liquor jumped by 400% at a time when the consumption of all kinds of alcohol by Canadians was down by half.

G. Donaldson and G. Lampert (eds.) *The Great Canadian Beer Book*, p. 5

BOOTLEGGERS

This Hamilton man smuggled liquor into Buffalo, New York, by strapping as many bottles to his body as he could, and then putting on his overcoat. Once he passed through customs, he could sell the bottles for $10 each.

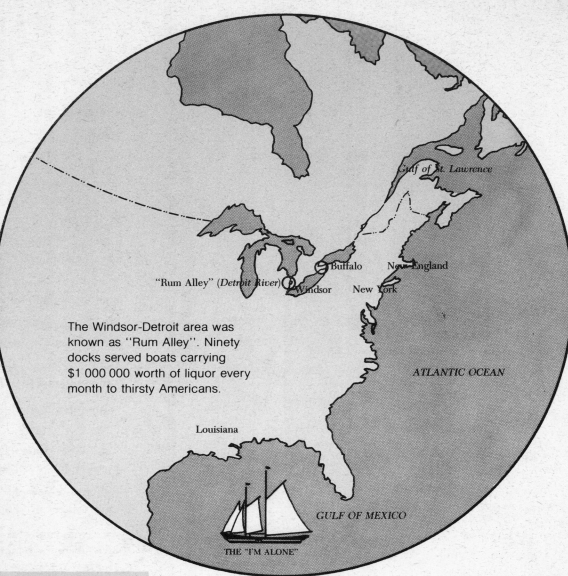

The Windsor-Detroit area was known as "Rum Alley". Ninety docks served boats carrying $1 000 000 worth of liquor every month to thirsty Americans.

THE "I'M ALONE"

THE "BIG SHOTS" OF BOOTLEGGING

Emilio "The Emperor Pick" Picariello worked out of Fernie, British Columbia. He had a fleet of cars which transported shipments of liquor through the Crow's Nest Pass into Alberta and then into the United States. "The Emperor Pick" paid bribes to police and provincial liquor agents. He was left alone until the Alberta government in 1922, cracked down on his operation. Eventually Picariello was arrested on a murder charge and hung May 3, 1923.

From *But Not in Canada* by Walter Stewart, published by the Macmillan Company of Canada Limited, 1976.

Rocco Perri operated out of Hamilton, Ontario with a fleet of cruisers and 40 trucks. Perri and his girlfriend, Bessie Starkman, organized a lucrative business of rum-running on the Great Lakes. But there was a price. Bessie was gunned down by rival mobsters in 1930 and Perri himself disappeared and was presumed dead in 1944.

The Canadian Magazine, Nov. 1, 1969

The "I'm Alone"

Canadian schooners smuggled whiskey to the coast of Louisiana, in the Gulf of Mexico, where their cargo was picked up by American speedboats, and transported inland. The Canadian ships could not be arrested by the United States Coast Guard as long as they remained outside of American territorial waters. In spite of this, in 1929, the "I'm Alone", a Nova Scotia rum-runner, was pursued and sunk by the United States Coast Guard in international waters.

A HOMEMADE STILL

1. fermented mash (potato or peach skins)
2. bath tub
3. electric hotplate or stove
4. copper kettle
5. copper tubing
6. jars for distilled brew

The dangers of bootleg booze were real: Every year throughout prohibition some Canadians died from drinking "rot gut".

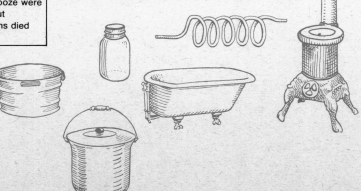

Officers destroy confiscated liquor.

LARGE SEIZURES OF LIQUOR MADE
87 Gallons of Alcohol Found on Macnab Street
Hamilton Spectator, June 1, 1925

WHAT TO DO WITH STOCK OF LIQUOR

Confiscated Intoxicants in Possession of the Police Are Now Causing Authorities Great Perplexity.

LAW IS NOT CLEAR AS TO ITS DISPOSITION

Regulations of Sale of Two Percent Beverages to Minors Is Also Attracting Serious Attention.

Would it be a breach of the prohibition act if the city police department sold the several thousand gallons of confiscated liquor now in their custody to the provincial liquor vendors?

Vancouver Sun, Apr. 17, 1929.

Female smuggler

STILL BUSTING TEMPERANCE ACT

RIVERS OF BEER RUNNING IN HOTELS OF MANITOBA CAPITAL; MOST BARS ARE "WIDE OPEN"

From three to six carloads a week, with an average of 60 barrels to the car, are being shipped into Saskatchewan by Manitoba brewers. This imported beverage, camouflaged as innocuous temperance drinks, varies in alcoholic content from 6 to 11 per cent. Its quantity and the widespread nature of the shipment to various portions of the province, constitutes a serious problem to the Saskatchewan authorities.

The *Leader*, in probing conditions in Winnipeg, made the discovery — that the open bar is a reality in Manitoba and [its capital city] Winnipeg... Strong beer is sold openly over the counter at 25 cents a glass; stronger drinks — mostly home brew — cost 50 cents a drink. This, too, is sold more or less openly in spite of the so-called "iron bound" temperance laws of Manitoba....

Regina Leader-Post, Dec. 22, 1922

HAMILTON MAN UNDER ARREST
Is Alleged to Have Been Toting Booze Cargo
Big Liquor Seizure in Tonawanda Hotel
Hamilton Spectator, June 1, 1925.

CONFESSIONS OF A BOOTLEGGER

"It found it very easy to make my own still — all you needed were some washtubs and coils of copper tubing. This was called a 'tea kettle' still and usually produced two gallons a day. The police had no way of stopping guys like me because the fines were too small. I heard about one bootlegger who was caught and fined $300. But the next day he was back in business earning over $7 000 a year from illegal booze.

"Besides, even if the government put all bootleggers out of business, a guy could always get a drink by doctor's prescription for 'medicinal purposes'."

CRIMINAL ACTS IN CANADA, 1928

	1926		1928	
Classes and Offences	Charges	Convictions	Charges	Convictions
	No.	No.	No.	No.
Class I. – Offences against the Person				
Murder	51	15	42	19
Murder, attempt to commit	13	7	21	18
Manslaughter	78	45	95	35
Shooting, stabbing and wounding	267	168	298	189
Aggravated assault	753	482	895	640
Assault on police officer	533	475	465	433
Assault and battery	1 487	1 261	1 576	1 283
Causing injury by fast driving	28	17	87	52
Various other offences against the person.	134	106	101	74
Class II. – Offences against Property with Violence				
Burglary, house, warehouse and shop breaking	1 711	1 417	2 175	1 948
Robbery and demanding with menaces	273	207	312	209
Highway robbery	2	1	13	10
Class III. – Offences against Property without Violence				
Embezzlement	10	6	9	8
False pretences	1 116	882	1 599	1 294
Feloniously receiving stolen goods.	604	400	596	398
Fraud and conspiracy to defraud	882	593	979	737
Horse, cattle and sheep stealing	53	37	61	48
Theft	8 139	6 651	9 479	7 870
Theft of mail	24	21	23	19
Theft of automobile	417	366	735	638
Class IV. – Malicious Offences against Property				
Arson	76	38	79	33
Malicious injury to horses and cattle, and other wilful damage to property	269	201	369	282
Class V. – Forgery and Other Offences against the Currency				
Offences against the currency	6	2	6	2
Forgery and uttering forged documents	451	383	627	549
Class VI. – Other Offences Not Included in the Foregoing Classes.				
Breach of the Trade Marks Act	49	48	26	26
Attempt to commit suicide	82	71	99	74
Carrying unlawful weapons	140	125	131	112
Criminal negligence	116	55	151	65
Conspiracy	135	53	100	49
Keeping bawdy houses and inmates thereof	831	739	918	844
Offences against gambling and lottery acts	590	550	1 524	1 403
Offences against revenue laws	233	193	330	240
Illicit stills	400	376	312	291
Perjury and subordination of perjury	107	60	139	70
Prison breach and escape from prison	162	152	166	155
Riot and affray	145	113	119	103

Canada Year Book 1928

Convictions for Offences against the Liquor Acts, years ended Sept. 30, 1900 – 1928:

Years	P.E.I.	N.S.	N.B.	Que.	Ont.	Man.	Sask.	Alta.	B.C.	Yukon.	N.W.T.	Total
1914	72	660	365	882	2 328	166	404	551	394	49	–	5 871
1915	42	633	390	1 021	2 018	124	378	573	246	27	–	5 452
1916	75	646	352	1 015	2 002	172	967	713	295	11	–	6 248
1917	36	449	312	1 076	2 927	289	774	885	576	15	–	7 339
1918	42	412	288	1 155	3 410	230	422	678	812	23	–	7 472
1919	37	479	387	1 479	3 353	175	434	436	597	6	–	7 383
1920	23	394	585	1 975	4 385	380	452	618	1 427	8	–	10 247
1921	44	362	419	1 384	4 938	427	583	907	1 394	2	–	10 460
1922	28	267	366	954	3 246	392	708	1 043	1 503	12	–	8 519
1923	39	264	364	1 724	3 958	542	997	990	1 196	14	–	10 088
1924	29	293	375	1 549	4 678	452	966	817	1 286	4	–	10 449
1925	51	235	319	1 919	5 047	512	1 078	758	1 699	9	9	11 636
1926	53	499	393	2 104	6 362	786	1 231	737	1 345	2	–	13 512
1927	66	610	271	2 025	5 620	627	1 245	814	1 186	13	–	12 477
1928	69	688	478	2 096	7 812	598	1 174	944	1 350	22	32	15 263

Canada Year Book, 1928

PLACES

A large percentage of Canadians lived in country or village settings such as this Gaspé fishing village. In the 1920s, the differences in speech, manner and dress between country and city folk were frequently quite pronounced. When the "city slicker" with his spiffy clothes visited the country or when the "rural hick", in his more functional attire, went to town, both stood a good chance of being the butt of numerous gibes.

Gaspé village

The railway was considered an essential part of modern living. Every large community had a railway yard in the most central, and quite often the most scenic, part of town, as in Ottawa pictured alongside. In other cities and towns if there was a river or a lake, the railway lines would quite often be located along the shoreline.

In the 1920s, countryside was close by, even when you travelled through the larger cities of Canada. If you couldn't see the country from your window as in this view of Dartmouth from Halifax, you needed only to travel a short distance to find the wide open spaces.

Ottawa skyline and railyards

CANADA'S URBAN POPULATION

Area	1921	1931
Canada	47.4%	52.5%
Maritimes	38.8	39.7
Prince Edward Island	18.8	19.5
Nova Scotia	44.8	46.6
New Brunswick	35.2	35.4
Quebec	51.8	59.5
Ontario	58.8	63.1
Manitoba	41.5	45.2
Saskatchewan	16.8	20.3
Alberta	30.7	31.7
British Columbia	50.9	62.3

Definition of Urban – pre 1951:
all incorporated cities, towns, villages.

Canada Year Book, 1931

SMALLER COMMUNITIES

		1921	1931
1.	Halifax	58 372	59 275
2.	Regina	34 432	52 209
3.	Victoria	38 727	39 082
4.	Stratford	14 877	18 191
5.	Charlottetown	10 814	12 261
6.	Medicine Hat	9 634	10 300
7.	St. Jerome	5 491	8 967
8.	Fredericton	8 114	8 830
9.	Cap de la Madeleine	6 738	8 798
10.	Portage la Prairie	6 766	6 597
11.	Edmunston, N.B.	4 035	6 436
12.	Springhill	5 681	6 355
13.	Nelson	5 230	5 992
14.	Weyburn	3 193	5 002

Dartmouth, Nova Scotia

TO LIVE

LARGE CITIES OF CANADA

1921		1931	
1. Montreal	618 506	1. Montreal	818 517
2. Toronto	521 893	2. Toronto	631 207
3. Winnipeg	179 087	3. Vancouver	246 593
4. Vancouver	117 217	4. Winnipeg	218 785
5. Hamilton	114 151	5. Hamilton	155 547
6. Ottawa	107 843	6. Quebec City	130 594
7. Quebec City	95 193	7. Ottawa	126 872
8. Calgary	63 305	8. Calgary	83 761
9. London	60 959	9. Edmonton	79 197
10. Edmonton	58 821	10. London	71 148

Looking up Granville St., Vancouver, B.C., 1914

Bonsecours Market, Montreal

Perhaps the best-known open-air farmers' market was Montreal's Bonsecours Market. Here a person could buy a wide variety of fresh produce sold by farmers from the surrounding area.

– A GROWING METROPOLIS –

"The city of Vancouver is so far away from Nova Scotia that we only know in a general way that it is quite a progressive community. Many will be surprised to know that it is becoming one of the most important ports on the continent.

"We usually think of Montreal as the big port of Canada where great tonnage calls in and out and tremendous quantities of freight inwards and outwards are handled, and it's a great port, leading in equipment and volume of business the great ports of the United States.

"But Vancouver is no mean competitor. Forty steamship lines now use the port of Vancouver. Its custom revenue is nearly one half of the revenue of Montreal. This is a striking fact when we remember the relatively large population served from Montreal."

Halifax Herald, November 13, 1922

ASSETS OF VANCOUVER – 1929

42	Banks	634	Apartment houses	8	Chiropodists
256	Manufacturers	245	Lawyers	41	Master plumbers
16	Palmists	232	Practicing physicians	2 949	Licenced dogs
10	Detective agencies	36	Chiropractors		

Vancouver *Province,* Jan. 5, 1929

MAIN STREET, 1923

Grocery Store
Drug Store
Jeweller
Dry Goods Store
Shoe Store
Theatre
Ice-Cream Parlour
Pool Hall

FACTS ABOUT TORONTO, 1926

106 630 people were employed in manufacturing.
.64 of people owned their own homes.
Largest annual exhibition in the world.
Approximately 225 000 000 letters sent out from Toronto Post Office in one year.
Residence lighting rate was less than $1 per month for a six-room house.
Best street lighting system in America and at the lowest cost.
More capital was invested in manufacturing in Toronto than in all the industries of British Columbia, Nova Scotia, and New Brunswick combined.

A Souvenir of Toronto, 1926, as quoted by M. Filey in *A Toronto Album: Glimpses of the City That Was,* p. 81

Granville St. looking north, Vancouver, B.C., 1927

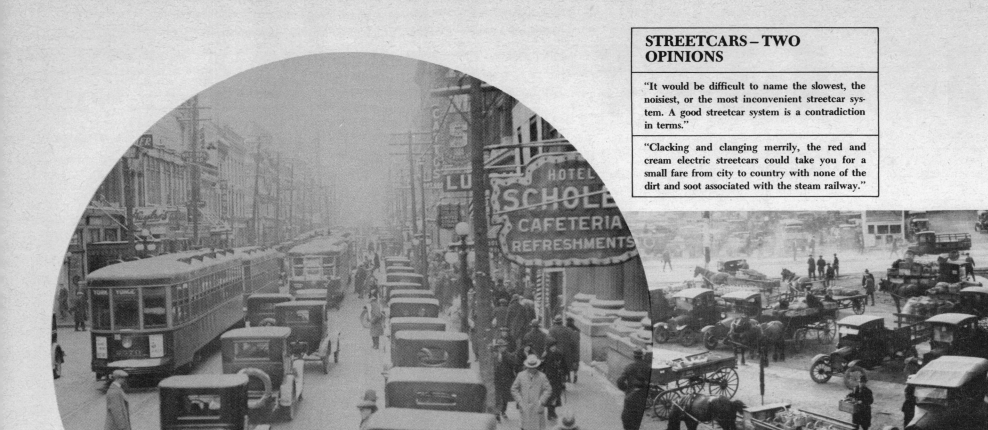

Yonge St., Toronto
The streetcar was a major source of transportation in many Canadian cities during the 1920s. This scene shows double streetcars in the pre-Christmas rush of 1924.

This vegetable market in Toronto near Humber Bay is shown as it was on August 31, 1923. Note the ratio of trucks to horse-drawn carts used by merchants and farmers.

ELECTRIC STREET RAILWAYS EXISTED IN 47 CANADIAN COMMUNITIES

Halifax, Moncton, Saint John, St. Stephen, Sydney, Yarmouth, St. John's, Hull, Lévis, Montreal, Quebec City, Sherbrooke, Trois Rivières, Belleville, Brantford, Cornwall, Fort William, Guelph, Hamilton, Kingston, Kitchener, London, Niagara Falls, Oshawa, Ottawa, Peterborough, Port Arthur, Sarnia, St. Catharines, St. Thomas, Sault Ste. Marie, Sudbury, Toronto, Waterloo, Welland, Windsor, Brandon, Calgary, Edmonton, Lethbridge, Moose Jaw, Nelson, Regina, Saskatoon, Vancouver (including North Vancouver and New Westminster), Victoria, and Winnipeg.

TRANSPORTATION: A TIME OF CHOICE

With the horse population in Canada peaking at 3.6 million in 1921, the horse was still widely-used for work on the farm and the distribution of goods. While the horse was a common sight for farm children, it provided a source of entertainment for city children: In summer, they could touch and feed the docile workhorse of the breadman, milkman, or iceman. In winter, the horse was a constant supplier of horse buns, which, when frozen, provided a serviceable and inexpensive puck for street hockey!

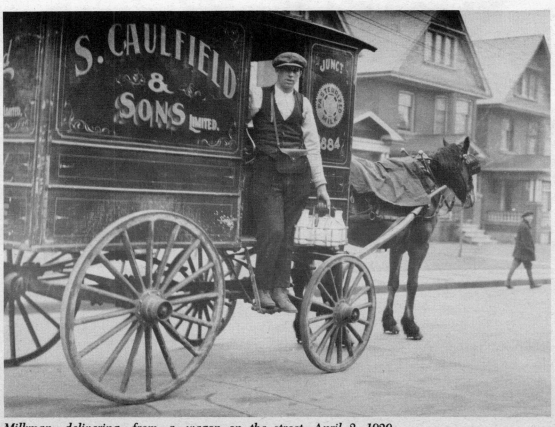

Milkman delivering from a wagon on the street, April 2, 1920

A SYMBOL OF CANADA

The Acadian, *Canadian National Railways, Beloeil, Quebec*

ARMAND BOMBARDIER

In his mid-teens, Joseph Armand Bombardier, frustrated by the isolation of winter snows in his hometown of Valcourt, Quebec put his early interest in machinery to work. After much trial and error, he constructed in 1926 his first reliable snowmobile consisting of the family sleigh, an automobile engine and an airplane prop.

Combining his mechanical creativity with a concern to provide heavy duty emergency transportation to snowbound northerners, he developed his first commercially successful snowmachine by 1936. Through dedication and skill, he formed and built up his own company Auto-Neige Bombardier Limitée to produce the present snowmobile which has become a vehicle of necessity and pleasure during the Canadian winter.

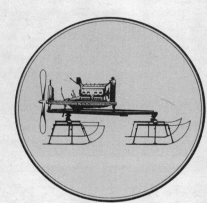

Armand Bombardier's first snowmobile

First Air Mail Flight

*September, 1927:
Montreal to Rimouski*
At Rimouski on the lower St. Lawrence, aircraft met transatlantic steamers to accelerate the mail for at least a part of its journey.

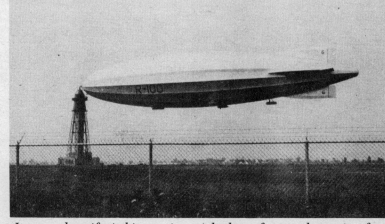

It seemed as if airship service might be a future alternative for long-distance travel. The British government selected Montreal as the western terminus of a service from Great Britain, and laid out a mooring base 16 km south of that city at St. Hubert in the years 1927-1930. The base was used once in the summer of 1930.

The steamer D.J. Purdy on its passenger route along the Saint John River, between Saint John and Fredericton, N.B., in 1920

THE AUTOMOBILE: INTRODUCING A WORLD OF VARIETY

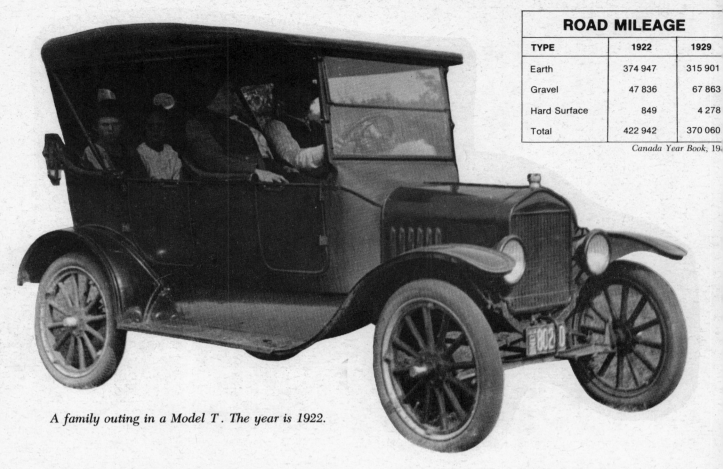

A family outing in a Model T. The year is 1922.

ROAD MILEAGE

TYPE	1922	1929
Earth	374 947	315 901
Gravel	47 836	67 863
Hard Surface	849	4 278
Total	422 942	370 060

Canada Year Book, 19..

Aids to Motoring

- Towrope
- Passengers
- Reverse gear
- Coal oil
- Electric light bulbs
- Shovels
- Tire chains
- Box of sand
- Automobile on blocks
- Horse and cutter

AUTOMOBILES OF CANADA IN THE 1920s

Models	City of Manufacture
Bourassa Six	Montreal
Brooks Steamer	Stratford
Chevrolet (General Motors)	Oshawa
Chrysler	Windsor
Derby	Saskatoon
Dodge (Part of Chrysler)	Toronto
Durant	Montreal
Ford	Windsor
Gray-Dort	Chatham
Hudson-Essex	Tilbury
Hupmobile	Windsor
Lavoie	Montreal
London Six	London
Maxwell (Renamed Plymouth)	Windsor
McLaughlin-Buick (General Motors)	Oshawa
Studebaker	Hamilton
Willys-Knight-Overland	Hamilton
Winnipeg	Winnipeg
Wright	Montreal

THE MODEL T FORD

The most common car was the mass-produced Model T Ford, which attracted buyers not so much for its often exaggerated durability as for its low purchase price and cheap maintenance. The combination of a high rate of sales and simplicity of design meant that new and used parts were quite inexpensive, and almost anyone could repair his own car. With its high clearance, the Model T also became the workhorse of the farmer, who employed the auto or its engine in many farm operations.

FEATURES – FORD MODEL T

Price: $495 in 1917; $424 in 1925
Power: 4 cylinder engine; 20 H.P. [14 914 W]
Weight: 540 kg
Top Speed: 64 km/h
Starter: Hand Crank
Gas Mileage: 8.9 km/L
Colour: Black (other colours extra)
Models: Touring, Sedan, Roadster, Coupe
Options: Spare tire, Windshield, Lights, Speedometer, Starter, Temperature gauge, Bumpers

Grant's Beach, Saskatchewan, c. 1928

Home of a returned soldier, Manitoba, 1920

A cream separator salesman and his wares

An automobile accident on Parkside Drive, Toronto, March 27, 1929

By 1928 one out of every two Canadian homes had an automobile.

Roadbuilding, 1920

The infamous prairie gumbo claims another victim, a hapless Alberta Model T. The sight of motorists struggling under such conditions was common in 1920, but became less frequent when roads improved.

SPEED LIMIT 1921

Open Country, km/h	
Prince Edward Island	24
Nova Scotia	40
New Brunswick	–
Quebec	40
Ontario	40
Manitoba	–
Alberta	–
British Columbia	48
Yukon	–

Canada Year Book, 1921

PERFORMANCE AND MAINTENANCE

Names like Ford and Chevrolet are familiar because they are still in production, but they were known in the 1920s as delicate cars. The Model T, operating on the principle that hot water rises, had no water pump. As a result, the oil thinned out at high speeds and caused the pistons or the main bearing of the engine to burn out.

Up to 1925, the weakness of the Chevrolet was a brittle axle. In the North, an owner would not drive his Chevy on a very cold day. If a family were out in the summer for a beach picnic, the Chevrolet was not driven in the sand, for this was a likely spot to break a back axle.

Other cars, such as the Gray-Dart and the Maxwell were considered more desirable . . . and more expensive. The Studebaker Six, a powerful and solid car, was popular with bootleggers for those 128 km/h "booze runs" from supplier to home market.

CONCERN FOR OTHERS

Churches had considerable influence within the 1920s communities, and whatever happened at church was a significant event. Here a Walkerton, Ontario dairy farm helps its workers attend a Sunday service in 1923.

Girl Guides at McDonald Point, New Brunswick

Y.M.C.A. fitness class, April, 1920

IMPORTANT CANADIAN ORGANIZATIONS

Canadian Boards of Trade in 1929
The Canadian Bar Association
Engineering Institute of Canada
Canadian Engineering Standards Association
The Canadian Institute of Mining and Metallurgy
Canadian Society of Technical Agriculturists
Association of Dominion Land Surveyors
Royal Canadian Institute
Royal Astronomical Society of Canada
The Canadian Authors' Association
Canadian Bible Society
The Canadian Teachers' Federation
National Conference of Canadian Universities
Canadian Federation of University Women·
Canadian Education Association
Canadian Political Science Association
The Canadian Red Cross Society
St. John Ambulance Association
The Canadian Nurses Association
The Victorian Order of Nurses
Royal College of Physicians and Surgeons of Canada
The Canadian Tuberculosis Association
Canadian National Committee for Mental Hygiene
Canadian National Institute for the Blind
Canadian Dental Association
Royal Canadian Humane Association
Canadian Cavalry Association
Canadian Artillery Association
The Canadian Legion
The Navy League of Canada
Amputations Association of the Great War
Last Post Fund
Canadian Credit Men's Trust Association
National Retail Credit Association

Dominion Commercial Travellers' Mutual Benefit Society
Canadian National Parks Association
Union of Canadian Municipalities
Exhibition Associations
Citizens' Research Institute of Canada
The Chief Constables' Association of Canada
National Council of the Y.M.C.A.
National Council of the Y.W.C.A.
The Women's Christian Temperance Union
The Boy Scouts Association
Canadian Girl Guides Association
The Social Service Council of Canada
National Boys' Work Board
The National Girls' Work Board
Big Brother Movement
Big Sister Movement
Canadian Council on Child Welfare
The Salvation Army
Association of Canadian Clubs
Canadian Club of New York
The Royal Empire Society (Montreal Branch)
The Empire Club of Canada
The Rotary Club
The Kiwanis Club
Native Sons of Canada
The National Council of Women
The Imperial Order Daughters of the Empire
Federated Women's Institutes of Canada
The Catholic Women's League of Canada
The Masonic Order
Orange Grand Lodge of British America
Knights Templar of Canada
Knights of Columbus
Canadian Order of Foresters
Order of the Mystic Shrine

The Canadian Annual Review of Public Affairs, 1928-29

GREAT HAILEYBURY FIRE: Oct. 4, 1922

An Appeal

For Relief For the

Northern Ontario Fire Sufferers!

10,000 sufferers in the fire scourged North appeal to you now for immediate relief.

10,000 men, women and little children, who have lost their homes, their employment, their clothing, their property, must be fed every day, must be clothed against the rigorous cold, must be temporarily sheltered — to give them a fighting chance a get on their feet again.

The Northern Ontario Fire Relief Committee

The Red Cross Is Cooperating With the Committee

Contributions of clothing, household equipment, etc., made in Toronto, may be sent to the Toronto Red Cross Emergency Depot at 94 Adelaide Street West, Toronto. Similar contributions from points outside Toronto may be made to the local Red Cross depots, or consigned direct to the Red Cross Commission at Cobalt, Ontario.

Only "Temporary Relief" Is Asked For

The Northern Relief Fire Committee does not rebuild homes, nor restock stores, nor erect public buildings. It simply feeds hungry children and men and women from day to day. It hopes to clothe the destitute adequately against the stark Northern cold. It hopes to provide some kind of temporary shelter amidst the blackened ruins, to give the helpless fire sufferers at least a fighting chance to re-establish themselves.

What Is the Northern Ontario Relief Committee?

It is a group of representative public and business men appointed by the Ontario Government to handle the relief work in connection with the terrible fires in the North Country in 1916. The Committee was authorized to continue to function by the Supreme Court of Ontario, and now has been asked by the Ontario Government to handle the present relief campaign. Over 110 000 pounds [49 895 kg] of groceries, 123 000 pounds [55 792 kg] of provisions, and great quantities of bedding and clothing have already been forwarded.

London Free Press, Oct. 14, 1922

DEADLY DISEASES

Typhoid fever	Pneumonia
Polio	Wound infections °
Diabetes	Scarlet fever °
Tuberculosis	Jaundice°
Perforated appendix	Diarrhoeal diseases °

° Children's diseases

TYPHOID FEVER EPIDEMIC

March – April 1927
Montreal
3 000 sick
200 deaths

J. I. Cooper, *Montreal: A Brief History*

MAJOR CHURCHES IN CANADA

CANADA 1921	8 787 949	Roman Catholic	3 399 011
Anglican	1 410 632	United, Presbyterian, Methodist	
Baptist	422 312	and Congregational	2 612 486
Jewish	125 445	Other denominations	531 172
Lutheran	286 891		*Census of Canada,* 1921

A COUNTRY DOCTOR

Mrs. K. had a sudden miscarriage at the fifth month of pregnancy. When I reached her home at 3 a.m. after a drive of six miles [9.6 km] on a cold winter night, she was unconscious at intervals from hemorrhaging. Her husband sidled up to me and said,

"Do the best you can, Doctor, we need her here." . . . The children were up and I could count – there were five.

Though I was prepared for this emergency I went outside to walk the road and think. My concern for the patient was compounded by a peculiar feeling of resentment. It was one of the few times I felt sorry for myself.

The house was on a hilltop and I could look about the countryside without a light visible for ten miles [16 km]. It was eerie. There I was, sweating out a problem in loneliness and anxiety when all about me people were enjoying sleep.

Suddenly Dr. Richardson's dictum came to me.

"No one can do better as there is no one else here."

I returned with a lighter heart to my patient . . .

William Victor Johnston MD, *Before the Age of Miracles: Memoirs of a Country Doctor,* pp. 14-15

Anglican mission at Montreal Lake, Saskatchewan, 1926

CAPE BRETON EARTHQUAKE

Epicentre – sea between Cape Breton and Newfoundland.

Destruction – Cape Breton, light
– isolated Burin Peninsula, south coast of Newfoundland
– 26 deaths, $2 000 000 damage
– $250 000 International Relief Fund.

QUAKE BORN TIDE DROWNS 26 *Nov. 18, 1929.*

Whole families perish as 50 foot [15.2 m] tidal wave sweeps homes into Newfoundland inlet.

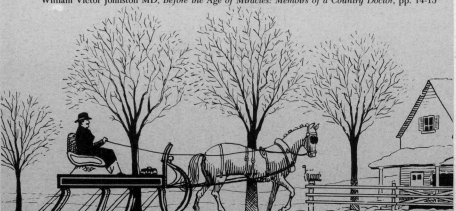

The country doctor

37

A Polish family settling at Ste. Anne, Manitoba, 1929

Canada: My Land of Opportunity

My name is John Corsorso. I was born in the North Italian community of Milan. I decided to settle in Kelowna, a small orchard city located on the seventy-mile stretch of Okanagan Lake in British Columbia. It was difficult at first because Kelowna had so many people of English background. I had many difficult times with the language and customs of Canadians. I was soon able to purchase some land of my own, which gave me great pride, because in Italy I worked land owned by other men. My crops of radishes, potatoes, onions and lettuce grew quickly. Later my wife joined me in Canada and proved to be of great help with the farm work. After years of hard work, I was able to buy more land and set up a retail shop in town. By the 1920s, I owned 20 000 acres and a shop which included a chilling plant, refrigerator and delicatessen counter. My wife and children shared my pride in our life in Canada.

Maclean's Magazine, Jan. 15, 1925

DESTINATIONS OF IMMIGRANTS INTO CANADA, BY PROVINCES

	Maritime Provinces	Quebec	Ontario	Manitoba	Sask-atchewan	Alberta	B.C. & Yukon Territory	Not shown	Totals
1919	3 860	6 772	13 826	4 862	8 552	11 640	8 190	—	57 702
1920	5 554	13 078	39 344	11 387	14 287	20 000	13 686	—	117 336
1921	6 353	21 100	62 572	12 649	13 392	17 781	14 630	—	148 477
1922	3 222	13 724	34 590	8 904	9 894	11 825	7 840	—	89 999
1923	3 298	9 343	30 444	6 037	8 186	8 798	6 781	—	72 887
1924	7 940	19 979	65 280	21 451	13 200	10 430	10 280	—	148 560
1925	3 153	16 279	45 912	11 772	14 041	10 952	9 253	—	111 362
1926	1 670	11 367	29 293	19 079	13 816	12 540	8 212	87	96 064
1927	3 125	16 642	40 604	36 739	20 085	16 367	10 410	16	143 991
1928	3 741	18 469	45 052	43 596	15 331	15 473	9 891	5	151 597

Canada Year Book, 1929

Kensington Market, Toronto, a meeting place of many nationalities

"Actual case studies in immigration do not always bear out theories based on the tabulation of figures by officials, or the deductions of experts. Last year a proposal in the Canadian parliament that only immigrants with money should be permitted entry was wrecked through the action of member after member who stood up and declared that he had come to this continent without a dollar. The same awkward intrusion of fact, offsetting fine-spun opinion, had similar results in the legislative bodies at Washington.

"Life histories are always valuable; in a study of immigration matters, particularly so. It is not often that they are found side by side in such a striking way as at Kelowna.

"Kelowna is a little orchard city lying midway down the seventy-mile stretch of Okanagan Lake in British Columbia. It is a Canadian town with an English atmosphere. Many of its people have hyphens in their names and family trees in their records. Among them are distinguished soldiers and retired legislators, men of wealth and women of culture. They have wonderful tennis courts and golf links, a club, and, before the war, power boats and yachts on the lake. Afternoon tea is a social rite. All the best-known London magazines are on the table at the club. English mail litters the secretaries of the private homes.

"But on this Canadian community with its superimposed English tone, two foreigners have left an impress of a marked kind." [One of them is John Corsorso:]
Maclean's Magazine, Jan. 15, 1925

COUNTRIES OF BIRTH OF IMMIGRANTS ARRIVING VIA OCEAN PORTS AND FROM THE UNITED STATES

Countries of birth	1927		
	Via Ocean Ports	From U.S.	Total
Canada	67	854	921
United States	378	15 928	16 306
England	22 949	1 211	24 160
Ireland	8 775	270	9 045
Scotland	14 340	651	14 991
Wales	1 771	46	1 817
Lesser British Isles	142	10	152
Newfoundland	958	34	992
St. Pierre and Miquelon	—	2	2
Mexico	24	6	30
Central America	4	1	5
Honduras (Br.)		1	1
Other South America	8	3	11
Argentina	16	3	19
Brazil	17	1	18
Chile	2	—	2
Guiana, British	17	1	18
West Indies (Br.)	116	28	144
West Indies (not Br.)	7	1	8
Austria	770	135	905
Belgium	2 204	45	2 249
Bulgaria	94	3	97
Czechoslovakia	6 659	26	6 685
Finland	5 800	38	5 838
France	358	42	400
Germany	2 012	188	2 200
Greece	358	31	389
Holland	1 485	54	1 539
Hungary	4 467	42	4 509
Italy	3 258	85	3 343
Yugo-Slavia	5 373	6	5 379
Poland	18 120	112	18 232
Rumania	2 555	49	2 604
Russia	6 602	333	6 935
Denmark	2 028	74	2 102
Iceland	31	7	38
Norway	3 355	284	3 639
Sweden	1 921	256	2 177
Switzerland	759	37	796
Ukraine	2 186	7	2 193
Albania	10	—	10
Estonia	84	—	84
Latvia	109	4	113
Lithuania	1 027	7	1 034
Malta	38	1	39
Portugal	5	—	5
Spain	22	4	26
Other European Countries including Luxemburg	25	2	27
Australia	187	23	210
New Zealand	97	11	108
Africa (Br.)	138	6	144
Africa (Not Br.)	13	6	19
Asia	35	3	35
Armenia	15	—	15
China	117	6	123
India (Br.)	199	10	209
Japan	492	1	493
Korea	6	—	6
Persia	13	—	13
Syria	214	12	226
Turkey	75	15	90
Atlantic Ocean Islands (Br.)	34	1	35
Atlantic Ocean Islands (not Br.)	25	8	33
Total	122 966	21 025	143 991

Canada Year Book, 1929

OPPORTUNITY... AND

Immigrants from central Europe arriving at Winnipeg, Manitoba, 1920s

PROHIBITED IMMIGRANTS

(1) Imbeciles, feebleminded persons, epileptics, insane persons, persons of constitutional psychopathic inferiority, persons suffering from chronic alcoholism and those mentally defective to such a degree as to affect their ability to earn a living.

(2) Persons afflicted with tuberculosis or with any loathsome, contagious or infectious disease, or a disease which may be dangerous to public health; immigrants who are dumb, blind or otherwise physically defective.

(3) Prostitutes and women and girls coming to Canada for any immoral purpose, pimps, procurers, and persons who have been convicted of any crime involving moral turpitude.

(4) Professional beggars or vagrants, charity-aided immigrants, and persons who are likely to become public charges.

(5) Anarchists, persons who disbelieve in or are opposed to organized government or who belong to any organization teaching disbelief in or opposition to organized government, persons who have been guilty of espionage or high treason, and persons who have been deported from Canada.

(6) Persons over fifteen years of age unable to read. The literacy test, however, does not apply to a father or grandfather over fifty-five years of age, or to a wife, mother, grandmother or unmarried daughter or widowed daughter.

Canada Year Book, 1929

The above is a summary of the classes whose admission to Canada was prohibited under the existing immigration regulation of the 1920s.

Doukhobors commemorate the anniversary of Peter Lordly Verigin's death, October 29, 1927, Brillant, B.C.

Ku Klux Klan meeting, Kingston, Ontario

KU KLUX MAN IN TOWN

"The new arrival reached London on Saturday afternoon from the Western States. The *Advertiser* witholds his name and rank, but has examined his credentials as a high official of the Imperial Ku Klux Klan, signed by Col. William Joseph Simmons of Atlanta, Georgia, founder of the order. The Imperial Klan is described as the central administrative body."

London Evening Advertiser, March 19, 1923.

"We feel that we are keeping well within the law in joining what we believe has been an unduly criticized organization on our continent. While we are anti-Jewish and anti-Negro, we shall not confine our actions to these sects and colours. Others who offend and who manage to evade the law better beware once we are properly organized."

Montreal Daily Star, Oct. 1, 1921.

The Ku Klux Klan of Kanada was organized during the late 1920s. It had thousands of members and exercised its greatest influence in Saskatchewan. The Klan concentrated its attack on Roman Catholics, Jews, and immigrants. It campaigned for Protestantism, racial purity, one public school, patriotism, and restrictive and selective immigration.

Number of Immigrants Coming to Canada

1919	107 698
1920	138 824
1921	91 728
1922	64 224
1923	133 729
1924	124 164
1925	84 907
1926	135 982
1927	158 886
1928	166 783
1929	164 993

"Good Outlook for Wheat Exports; Continuance of European Demand Will Absorb All but Sixty Million Bushels°".

1905-1911	1912-1918	1919-1925
5 737 255 BUSHELS	120 174 400 BUSHELS	183 777 423 BUSHELS

°there is no metric equivalent for bushels

Saturday Night, Aug. 20, 1926

Occupations and Destinations of Immigrants arriving in Canada in the fiscal year ended March 31, 1927

DESCRIPTION	Via Ocean Ports	From the United States	Totals
Farmers and farm labourers—			
Men	55 650	5 233	60 883
Women	5 460	1 203	6 663
Children	12 717	1 691	14 408
General labourers—			
Men	4 862	1 323	6 185
Women	847	224	1 071
Children	1 454	205	1 659
Mechanics—			
Men	4 617	1 775	6 391
Women	1 562	398	1 960
Children	1 184	303	1 487
Clerks, traders, etc.—			
Men	2 105	978	3 083
Women	1 064	362	1 426
Children	663	186	849
Miners—			
Men	965	151	1 116
Women	104	10	114
Children	127	7	134
Domestics—			
Women[1]	13 019	538	13 557
Not classified—			
Men	1 564	1 240	2 854
Women	7 592	2 445	10 037
Children	7 410	2 704	10 114
Totals—			
Men	69 763	10 749	80 512
Women[1]	29 648	5 180	34 828
Children	23 555	5 096	28 651
Totals	122 966	21 025	143 991
Destination—			
Maritime Provinces	2 738	387	3 125
Quebec	13 735	2 907	16 642
Ontario	34 769	5 835	40 604
Manitoba	35 469	1 290	36 739
Saskatchewan	16 423	3 662	20 085
Alberta	11 780	4 587	16 367
British Columbia	8 060	2 316	10 376
Yukon and N.W.T.	4	30	34
Not given	8	11	19

[1] Includes domestics under 18 years of age.

Canada Year Book, 1929

ONE COLOR FOR ENTIRE COSTUME

FOREIGN INFLUENCES

Halifax Herald, Nov. 13, 1922

The larger New York shops report a tendency for well-dressed women to choose underwear that not only corresponds in line to their outer garments but that corresponds in color as well.

To accompany evening gowns, besides the usual white and pink, there are shades of orange, American beauty, cerise, lavender, blue and green. Many sets are elaborately trimmed with dyed laces.

Black underwear is shown, as well as brown and navy blue for day-time wear with dark frocks. Knee-length bloomers are replacing those of ankle-length, to make way for the recently returned petticoats of the new costume slip.

This window display of the Hoover vacuum cleaner on Sparks St., Ottawa, in February, 1920, was a good example of the growing input of American design, production, and marketing

FILMS PRODUCED IN CANADA

"Another potent influence for bringing Canada into spiritual subjection to the United States is the moving picture show. The films are made for American audiences, naturally, to suit their tastes. Then they come to Canada. We originate none practically." Archibald MacMechen, Professor of English, Dalhousie University, Halifax, 1920

Canadian Films, 1919-1929

1.	Back To God's Country	1919	13.	The Man from Glengarry	1922
2.	Satan's Paradise	1920	14.	Proof of Innocence°	1922
3.	Under Northern Lights	1920	15.	The Rapids	1922
4.	The Vow°	1920	16.	Policing the Plains°	1922
5.	Cameron of the Royal Mounted	1921	17.	The Swiling Racket°	1927
6.	Campbell of the Mounted°	1921	18.	Carry on, Sergeant°	1928
7.	God's Crucible	1921	19.	His Destiny	1928
8.	Latin Love	1921	20.	The Wilderness Patrol	1928
9.	Snowblind	1921	21.	The Devil Bear°	1929
10.	Valley of the Missing°	1921	22.	Race for Ties°	1929
11.	Blue Water°	1922	23.	Spirit of Wilderness°	1929
12.	The Critical Age	1922	24.	The White Road°	1929

°No record of release or unsuccessful release.   Canadian Film Institute

16 Old Time Favorite Songs $2.98 For All

Eight Double-Disc Full Size 10 inch Records

In The Gloaming
Auld Lang Syne
Ben Bolt
Old Black Joe
Love's Old Sweet Song
Kathleen Mavourneen
Comin' Through the Rye
My Old Kentucky Home
Old Folks at Home
Home, Sweet Home
Sweet and Low
Lullaby (Erminie)
Nearer My God To Thee
Annie Laurie
Last Rose of Summer
Schubert's Serenade

Here are the songs that never grow old—the favorites you remember as long as you live, ballads that touch every heart. Just the music that should be in EVERY HOME. Eight full size double face records—16 wonderful old time songs—quality guaranteed equal to highest priced records—All for only $2.98. Can be played on any phonograph.

Send No Money. Try these records in your own home for 10 days. If not delighted the trial costs nothing. Don't send a penny now. Pay postman only $2.98 plus postage on arrival. Money back at once absolutely guaranteed if you are not more than pleased. Write postal or letter NOW.

National Music Lovers, Inc., Dept. 1563, 354 Fourth Av. New York

Everywoman's World, March, 1923

DAILY COMIC STRIPS

"Take the most potent influence at work on the popular mind, our journalism. Hundreds of thousands of Canadians read nothing but the daily newspaper. Not only is the Canadian newspaper built on American lines but it is crammed with American boilerplate of all kinds, American illustrations, American comic supplements."

Archibald MacMechen, Professor of English,
Dalhousie University, Halifax, 1920

POPULAR COMIC STRIPS

1.	Bringing Up Father	Great Britain
2.	Gasoline Alley	United States
3.	Toots and Casper	Great Britain
4.	Polly and her Pals	Great Britain
5.	Tillie the Toiler	Great Britain
6.	Winnie Winkle the Breadwinner	United States
7.	Mutt and Jeff	United States
8.	Bonzo	Great Britain
9.	Son of Tarzan	United States
10.	Little Orphan Annie	United States
11.	Keeping up with the Joneses	United States

Toronto Star, Dec. 1929

Lawn bowlers, Uxbridge Bowling Green, July 11, 1923

Why Canada should prohibit the export of power and pulpwood....

Because our people are following Canadian raw materials south.

TRADE 1929 (MILLIONS OF $)	
TOP TWELVE IMPORTS BY VALUE	
1. Machinery	$60
2. Automobile parts	56
3. Coal	55
4. Spirits and wines	58
5. Automobiles	42
6. Farm implements	40
7. Crude petroleum	39
8. Plates and sheets (iron)	31
9. Raw cotton	28
10. Electric apparatus	27
11. Sugar for refining	26
12. Green fruits	25
TOTAL IMPORTS .. $1 265 679 000	

TOP TWELVE EXPORTS BY VALUE	
1. Wheat	$428
2. Printing paper	142
3. Wheat flour	65
4. Planks and boards	48
5. Wood pulp	45
6. Automobiles	43
7. Fish	34
8. Copper ore and blister	27
9. Barley	26
10. Cheese	25
11. Raw furs	24
12. Whiskey	24
TOTAL EXPORTS $1 388 896 000	

Canada Year Book, 1930

EMIGRATION

Nova Scotia

"[After World War I], a drift of population to the United States set in at once. By 1925, it was an exodus. A large and significant proportion of these departing people were young veterans of the war."

T. Raddall, *Warden of the North*

Quebec

To find employment to pay off farming debts, many farmers went to the mills of New England where wages were higher. Although many Québécois returned after 3 or 4 months, a good number remained in the United States permanently.

Ontario

"In Southwestern Ontario, we were taught that Canadian patriotism should not withstand anything more than a $5 – a – month wage differential. Anything more than that and you went to Detroit."

J. K. Galbraith, quoted from "Canada's Boundaries: A Study of Anomalies", by J. Eayrs, *London Free Press*, July 1, 1976

Pulp and Paper

Canadian-based companies controlled 64% of the world's pulp and paper trade in the 1920s.

A. B. Hodgetts, *Decisive Decades*, p. 313

Oil

In the 1920s 95% of Canada's oil was imported.

A. B. Hodgetts, *Decisive Decades*, p. 309

PETEY   Is She Stringing Him?   By C. A. VOIGHT

Manitoba Free Press, August 6, 1927, © New York Tribune, Inc., 1927

THE CONQUEST OF THE NORTH

In 1927, the Canadian Government began to develop air mail service to the North, constructing airstrips, mapping out air routes, and encouraging the development of suitable equipment. On December 28, 1929, the first air mail arrived at Aklavik.

Aklavik

Mackenzie River

Cambridge Bay

Fort Norman

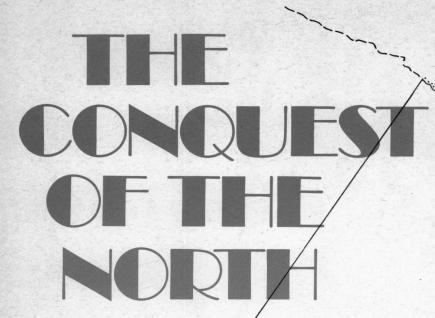

Wreck of the Curtiss aircraft Polar Bear in Prince Rupert, B.C., September 28, 1921

Fort Smith

Fort Vermilion

BRITISH COLUMBIA

ALBERTA

SASKATCHEWAN

MANITOBA

Fort McMurray

Edmonton

A Bushpilot's Diary

There are lots of great pilots flying in the North today – men like 'Punch' Dickens, 'Wop' May, 'Doc' Oates. We all make many stops on the Edmonton to Aklavik route, usually in severe weather. We have few instruments in the cockpit, so we fly 'by the seat of our pants'. We often use landmarks to guide us. Landing is always treacherous – in the summer, the planes are fitted with pontoons to land on lakes, and in winter, fitted with skis to land on the ice. There are routine flights to transport mail, supplies, R.C.M.P. officers, prospectors and mining company officials. But there are lots of emergency flights. 'Wop' May flew anti-toxin up to Fort Vermilion to combat a diptheria epidemic. Two pilots, Blasdale and Vance, crashed near Baker Lake while searching for the lost McAlpine party. They had to stay at an isolated trading post until the weather cleared.

```
1926 – 44 bush planes
1928 – 264 bush planes
```

Imperial Oil Limited and other companies drilled for oil in Alberta. The most successful discovery was at Fort Norman. A natural gas well was also found in Turner Valley.

DR. MACMILLAN SETS OUT AGAIN FOR THE ARCTIC

HARTFORD, Conn., June 21, (Copyright)—That the wireless apparatus on the *Bowdoin*, the tiny schooner which is carrying Dr. Donald B. MacMillan and his party to the Arctic, is in fine working order, was demonstrated today by the receipt by hundreds of amateur stations throughout the country of a message from the ship. Reports of this communication were received at the Radio Relay League headquarters here. In spite of bad static, the fading words sent by Donald H. Mix, the twenty-one year old wireless operator on board the *Bowdoin*, were clearly heard.

At the conclusion of the text many of the amateurs called Mix indicating that the signals were strong and that there is an excellent chance of direct communication to the furthest Arctic regions.

The *Bowdoin* announced the fact that she has put into Booth Bay Harbour and leaves for Halifax on Monday morning.
Halifax Herald, June 25, 1923

Imperial Oil Limited expedition to Norman Oil Fields, 1921

RADIO KEEPS TOUCH WITH ARCTIC WASTES

Remarkable Results Are Reported by Explorer
Says Eskimos and Missionaries Listen In
Canadian Press Service

Arlington Heights, Ill., Aug. 6,—News interviews by personal contact and other ordinary, domestic means, today gave way to the romance of radio, when the Associated Press interviewed the MacMillan polar expedition 3 700 miles away in the Arctic wastes.

Lieut. Commander Eugene F. McDonald of the *Peary* which conveyed the expedition to its base in Etah, Greenland, answered a series of five questions radioed to him by the Associated Press.

COMMUNICATION WITH PLANES
The outstanding questions dealt with the future flight of airplanes to the polar region from Etah; McDonald replied, that he had not yet completed "two-way communication" with big planes, but hoped to perfect such communication. His reply was regarded here as being a plan to communicate continually with his planes while they were in the air northward from Etah.

Communication was first established last night with the expedition about ten o'clock central daylight saving time.

"Station WAP—Etah," said the announcer, whose voice seemed to be smothered by a snow drift—and the remainder of his voice was lost in an indistinguishable, mumbled monotone. Shortly thereafter a squeaky, then somewhat clearer tone came through, which was finally recognized as phonograph music.

Hamilton Spectator, Aug. 6, 1925

The Arctic work is becoming increasingly important; there are now in the Arctic and sub-Arctic regions (exclusive of the Yukon) 33 detachments with 91 all ranks, or about 9% of the entire strength. These detachments include posts on Ellesmere, North Devon, Baffin and Victoria Islands, as well as along the coasts of the Arctic Ocean and Hudson Bay; one (Bache Peninsula) is within eleven degrees of the North Pole, and a powerful auxiliary power schooner, the *St. Roch*, employed in the Arctic Ocean, ranks as a detachment; every winter long patrols are made in these regions, the islands west of Ellesmere Island (Axel Heiberg, etc.) being visited periodically. Contrasted with this is detective work in the urban communities, in running to earth counterfeiters, narcotic drug dealers, robbers of the mails, and others of the more dangerous types of evildoers.

Canada Year Book, 1929.

"A new sound broke that same chill silence—the drone of the first aeroplane to cross the skies of the North-West Territories, a Junkers machine of the Imperial Oil Company, flying northward to Fort Simpson. It entered the Territories on March 27th, and in it, acting as guide, was Thorne, returning from Edmonton—a veteran Sergeant of the Old Force appropriately ushering in the New Regime.
And making 'the first aeroplane journey on duty in the annals of the Force'."

Col. H. Steele, *Policing the Arctic*, p. 225

"Ice conditions near Dundas Harbour were still so dangerous (a native hunter had been all but carried off in January) that, as a preliminary to Joy's forthcoming patrol, it was thought advisable for Corporal Timbury to go beforehand to Beechey to observe the state of the ice in Lancaster Sound and to examine the cache. He left on February 12th with Nookapeeungwak and another native. The ice was very rough, broken here and there by leads, but negotiable. The cache was found intact. In spite of storms they were back at Dundas on the 28th.
Two days before, Dersch had started a 1 133-mile [1 818km], forty-eight-day journey westward from Lake Harbour to Amadjuak, Cape Dorset and Cape Dorchester, a pioneer 'general purpose' patrol carried out with his usual skill."

Col. H. Steele, *Policing the Arctic*, p. 295

Policing the Arctic: The Story of the Conquest of the Arctic by the Royal Canadian Mounted Police
by
Col. Harwood Steele

"The first murder-trial in the area still known as the North-West Territories opened on June 29th (while Phillips was revisiting the Belcher Islands, with relief, and Bruce on a 4 000-mile journey with the makers of Treaty No. 11, covering the Mackenzie and Great Slave Lake). It had been decreed that Le Beaux should be tried at Fort Providence. His Honour Judge Lucien Dubuc made the journey from Edmonton for the purpose. Six jurymen, five from Fort Smith, heard the case. All arrangements were in Fletcher's capable hands.
"The accused was found guilty and sentenced to hang at Fort Smith on November 1st, 1921."

Col. H. Steele, *Policing the Arctic*, p. 225

SCHEDULE	Headquarters Staff	Maritime Provinces	Québec	Ontario	Manitoba	Saskatchewan	Alberta	British Columbia	Yukon	Northwest Territories	Baffin Island	Ellesmere Island	North Devon Island	Chesterfield Inlet	On Loan	Canada
Total Canada 1929	64	34	39	316	57	352	112	88	43	75	7	3	3	5	1	1 199
Total Canada 1928	68	35	35	298	49	262	123	88	41	71	7	3	4	–	3	1 087
Total Canada 1927	69	36	36	306	54	170	112	99	39	65	8	3	3	–	4	1 004
Total Canada 1926	66	28	37	276	47	173	113	93	34	56	7	3	3	–	27	963
Total Canada 1925	72	30	27	294	52	182	116	94	37	49	8	3	3	–	10	977
Total Canada 1924	72	32	27	295	51	192	128	109	40	52	7	2	3	–	10	1 020
Total Canada 1923	72	32	31	317	64	253	152	143	42	29	4	9	–	–	–	1 148
Total Canada 1922	79	37	41	288	71	274	173	175	51	27	4	7	–	–	–	1 227
Total Canada 1921	79	32	26	440	162	329	266	265	52	28	1	–	–	–	–	1 680
Total Canada 1920	72	25	9	384	160	400	300	257	48	16	–	–	–	–	–	1 671

Strength and Distribution of the Royal Canadian Mounted Police on Sept. 30, 1929 with Totals on Sept. 30, 1920-29

Canada Year Book, 1929

However ... The Plight of Inuit

An Inuit hunter is taken into custody by an R.C.M.P. officer stationed in the North. There were conflicts between the laws of the native Inuit and the laws of the white man.

According to Dr. D. E. Scott, who recently returned to Edmonton after spending one year at the delta of the Mackenzie River, the Eskimos are doomed to extinction within a few years through disease brought on by the adoption of the white man's ways of living. Dr. Scott has been acting as a medical officer to the Royal Canadian Mounted Police stationed at these far northern points and his duties also included the medical care of the local Indians and Eskimos on behalf of the Department of Indian Affairs. He therefore has had the very best opportunity for studying conditions. His report does not stand alone, either. All competent observers are agreed that the natives of the Arctic regions are deteriorating to an alarming extent, physically, on account of the change which has been brought about in their habits of life, in the matter of food and habitation especially, since their contact with civilization. Stefansson, in his fascinating account *The Friendly Arctic*, gives the same information. He sketches the healthy, happy, and care-free condition of the Eskimo in his former unsophisticated way of life. The native knew well how to take care of his health and his well-being. His icehouses were warm...; his clothing was perfectly adapted to the requirements of his environment. Now there is an attempt to [imitate] the white people in everything: the primitive igloo has been abandoned for the more pretentious, but much more unsatisfactory wooden hut: the style of clothing has been changed with disastrous results to health, and, more important still, there has been a change of diet and habits which has wrought havoc with the natives. Dr. Scott speaks of the prevalence of cancer, appendicitis, intestinal trouble and, above all, tuberculosis, induced by changed methods of living—and all these diseases are alarmingly on the increase.

Hamilton Spectator, July 29, 1925

Inuit family

43

CANADA BECOMES A NATION

The national flag for Canada proposed by Col. J. F. Mitchell

"In presenting this design for a Canadian flag, I am not advocating Canada should have a distinctive flag, or should substitute [it for] Union Jack. But recognizing there is a deep and growing sentiment f national flag in Canada, I believe it better to guide that sentiment in right direction."

Col. J. F. Mitchell, Speech in
Canadian House of Commons,

Rt. Hon. W. L. Mackenzie King
Lib. 1921 - 1926 ; 1926 - 1927

Mr. Mackenzie King:

"Especially in the case of the younger and smaller countries, foreign relations are mainly neighbourhood relations. It is with neighbours as a rule that intercourse is most frequent, and the number of difficulties requiring joint adjustment is greatest. It is not surprising, therefore, that in Canada, foreign relations mean predominantly relations with the United States. The United States is very much our neighbour, sharing a common border line over three thousand miles in length, and the relationship is intensified by the comparative absence of other near neighbours. It is not an unmixed blessing to have a neighbour so dominant in wealth and population and ambition, but there is certainly no other great foreign power we would as soon have at our doors.

"I have found some apprehension as to the Americanisation of Canada. Certainly our business and social relations are very close, and are bound to be closer, and many phases of our life reflect United States influence. But, so far as there is similarity of attitude, it is as likely to be due to similarity of New World conditions as to the influence of one country or the other, and in fundamentals there is no evidence or likelihood of United States permeation [influence]. We are developing not only a distinct national consciousness, as Lord Byng indicated the other evening, which serves as the strongest possible safeguard against such permeation [influence], but a distinct national type of character and of social organization which our friends of the United States are the first to note and recognize. Social absorption, I may assure the pessimists, is as far off as political union."

– Prime Minister Mackenzie King, Imperial Conference, October 25, 1926
Documents on Canadian External Relations, 1926-1930, Vol. IV

FLAGS
For All Occasions

Cotton Flags on sticks. Wool Bunting Flags with toggle to fasten to pole rope. Prices for special sizes. Silk or Wool on application. COTTON FLAGS, sizes as below, are Union Jacks Canadian, French.

The Archives, Eaton's of Canada, Ltd.

1922 Chanak

1919 Peace Conference

"Canada had led the democracies of both the American continents. Her resolve had given inspiration, her sacrifices had been conspicuous, her effort was unabated to the end. The same indomitable spirit which made her capable of that effort and sacrifice made her equally incapable of accepting at the Peace Conference, in the League of Nations, or elsewhere, a status inferior to that accorded to nations less advanced in their development, less amply endowed in wealth, resources, and population, no more complete in their sovereignty, and far less conspicuous in their sacrifice."

—*Prime Minister Robert Borden*, 1919

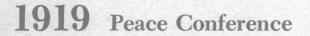

The Globe.
98,639

VOL. LXXIX   NUMBER 22,690   TORONTO, FRIDAY, SEPTEMBER 7th 1922   30 PAGES

TURKS SURROUND BRITISH TROOPS IN CHANAK AREA
KEMAL'S FORCES OVERRUN NEUTRAL ZONE ON ASIATIC SIDE OF STRAITS OF DARDANELLES AND ARE UP AGAINST BRITISH ENTRENCHMENTS

From the *Globe*, by permission of
The Globe and Mail, Toronto

Chanak Crisis

After the First World War, Britain occupied positions at the straits leading from the Black Sea to the Mediterranean. Turkey, which had been on the losing side in the First World War, decided to seize control of the area, which was, in fact, within Turkish territory. It sent in troops, and Britain sent troops and ships to defend the area around Chanak against Turkey. The British Government sent a cable to Ottawa requesting that Canadian troops be sent to the area to help in the defence. However, an official in London gave the information contained in the cable to members of the Canadian Press, hoping to embarrass the Canadian Government into sending help.

Prime Minister Mackenzie King responded: "I confess it annoyed me. . . . Surely all that has been said about equality of status and sovereign nations within the Empire is all of no account if at any particular moment the self-governing Dominions are to be expected, without consideration of any kind, to assume the gravest responsibility which a nation can assume [going to war]. No Canadian contingent [troops] will go [to Chanak] without Parliament being summoned in the first instance. I shall not commit myself one way or the other. . . . I am sure the people of Canada are against participation in this European war."

For the first time, Canada was not automatically at war when England was.

ENDORSES PLAN OF DISTINCTIVE CANADIAN FLAG

Founder of First Club Tells Of Movement
Subject Was Given Attention Thirty Years Ago
Pleased That Ottawa Is Acting at Last

A subject that has been occupying the mind of Col. C. R. McCullough, of this city, for the last thirty years, is now attracting nationwide attention. When the colonel formed the Canadian Club thirty years ago, he and the others who were active in the movement agitated for a distinctive Canadian flag, that would be made the official emblem of Canada. A few days ago Parliament appointed a committee of Deputies to go into the matter of a flag for Canada. The idea is to have suggestions sent to this committee from patriotic bodies all over the country. After due consideration, the selection will be made, and Canada will have an official flag at last.

The emblem in use at the present time consists of the British red ensign, with the official coat-of-arms of Canada on the fly. It is flown over the High Commissioner's office in London, and is generally accepted as the Canadian flag. It is really not official, though, and came into use through the Canadian merchant marine. Long ago Canadian merchant ships started to use the red naval ensign, so the practice of using the ensign with the coat-of-arms came into being.

Hamilton Spectator, June 11, 1925

ONE FLAG

There will be much sympathy for the viewpoint of the Imperial Order Daughters of the Empire regarding the proposal of the Dominion Government to devise a new flag for Canada. "One flag, one throne, one Empire," is a slogan with the I.O.D.E., and it is an excellent motto for adoption by the whole Empire. The ties binding the dominions together are ties of sentiment only, and there is no greater agent for the knitting of sentiment than a common flag. What could have persuaded the government that the present is a convenient time for bringing in this suggestion is hard to understand. Just now, when the Mother Country is wondering exactly what is meant by Canada's constant and somewhat vigourous assertions of independence, is scarcely the appropriate occasion for giving cause for further speculation.

This loyal Dominion feels humiliated by a succession of incidents which, however lacking in significance in themselves, are giving the impression abroad that the bonds of Empire are growing weaker and that Canada is impatient to cut the painter. No sensible Canadian is desirous of setting the country adrift in this way, of course: the affection and admiration for the Mother Land which prevail to-day in this British Dominion are perhaps stronger than ever before. But those in authority have the strangest way of demonstrating the fact. No opportunity is missed of asserting our national autonomy. There is, of course, not the slightest dispute as to that autonomy: but good taste, if nothing else, should prevent undue emphasis.

The facts are that we are all very, very proud of the Empire, proud of our ancestry and traditions, proud of the great and noble Mother Land, whose honorable reputation to-day stands at its zenith, and proud of the Union Jack which is the symbol of her power and authority. Under that flag we live secure and free, British in thought and heart and in our mode of living. This same flag unites the various elements of the country in one common sentiment and aspiration. Canada is inseparable from Britain and the Empire, and the Union Jack is the sign of that inseparability. "Quis separabit?" Let us jealously guard the precious emblems of our unity. The community owes a debt of gratitude to the I.O.D.E. for its patriotic action in this matter.

Hamilton Spectator, June 11, 1925

EMPIRE DAY

Joined with these is our old English ensign,
St. George's red cross on white field;
Round which, from Richard to Roberts,
Britons conquer or die, but ne'er yield.

It flutters triumphant o'er ocean,
As free as the wind and the waves;
And bondsmen from shackles unloosened,
'Neath its shadows no longer are slaves.

It floats o'er Australia, New Zealand,
O'er Canada, the Indies, Hong Kong;
And Britons, where'er their flag's flying,
Claim the rights which to Britons belong.

We hoist it to show our devotion
To our King, our country, and laws;
It's the outward and visible emblem,
Of progress and liberty's cause.

You may say it's an old bit of bunting,
You may call it an old coloured rag;
But freedom has made it majestic,
And time has ennobled our flag.

1923 Halibut Treaty

Treaty Between Canada and the United States of America For Securing the Preservation of the Halibut Fishery of the North Pacific Ocean.

Signed at Washington March 2, 1923.

His Majesty the King of the United Kingdom of Great Britain and of the British Dominions, and the United States of America, being equally desirous of securing the preservation of the halibut fishery of the North Pacific Ocean have resolved to conclude a Convention for this purpose, and have named as their plenipotentiaries: His Britannic Majesty; The Honourable Ernest Lapointe, Minister of Marine and Fisheries of Canada; and Charles Evan Hughes, Secretary of State of the United States.

Treaties and Agreements Affecting Canada 1814-1925

1926 Imperial Conference

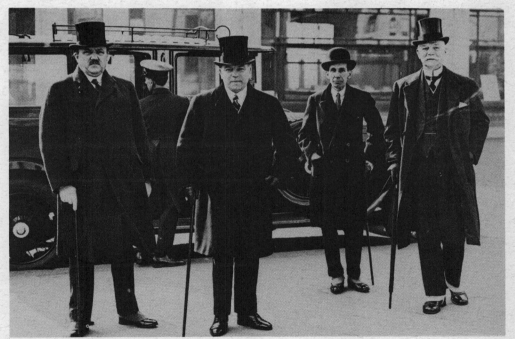

Prime Minister Mackenzie King at the Imperial Conference of 1926

At the Imperial Conference, a committee under the chairmanship of Lord Balfour, drafted a major report in which it was stated: "The dominions are autonomous communities within the British Empire, equal in status, in no way subordinate to one another in any aspect of their domestic or external affairs, though united to a common allegiance to the Crown and freely associated as members of the British Commonwealth of Nations."

THE DOOR TO THE FUTURE

Today there are prophets—more than at any time in the world's history.

They are found in big business institutions, for big institutions are built on the faith and vision of far-seeing men. While other men around them work in 1925, these business prophets work, by habit of thought and training, in the future—five, ten, yes, twenty or twenty-five years ahead of the times.

They are the men who are planning new applications of science and industry: perfecting new processes, new products, new appliances,—not for today, but for the time when public service will demand them. In the research department of the Northern Electric Company there is a door through which the men of this engineering organization are always trying to peer.

It is the door to the Future Electrical Age.

Our products of today are the result of their efforts in peering through that door. Products which will appear on the market perhaps tomorrow, perhaps five or ten years hence—these have already crossed the vision of the prophets who peered through that magic door and saw the needs of this and future generations.

Northern Telecom Limited
Maclean's Magazine, Nov. 15, 1925.

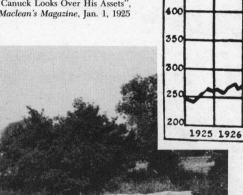

"...Mr. and Mrs. John Canuck have been given a comfortable home, with all the modern conveniences, pantries stocked with food, coal in the cellar and a motor car waiting on the side drive. All Jack Canuck needs is a job, with wages, to keep the home going.

"Of income, however, he has ample for comfort if he will avoid over-indulgence in luxuries. The cardinal virtues are invariably the backbone of a country: hard work and economy."

J. Herbert Hodgins, "Johnny Canuck Looks Over His Assets",
Maclean's Magazine, Jan. 1, 1925

"The Dawn of a New Year"

"Johnny Canuck, giving his vast resources a satisfied once-over, presents a cheerful, stimulating picture. Johnny Canuck is not dominated by selfish interest. He loves gold for what gold will do for humanity. He surveys his country richly endowed, and sighs for more people to come and share his treasure."

J. Herbert Hodgins, "Johnny Canuck Looks Over His Assets",
Maclean's Magazine, Jan. 1, 1925

A free auto laundry in the Humber River, Lambton, Ont., October 29, 1929

NATION'S BUSINESS

83% of Canada's business was done by 1 000 Corporations.

A. B. Hodgetts, *Decisive Decades,* p. 321

A rural home in Nova Scotia

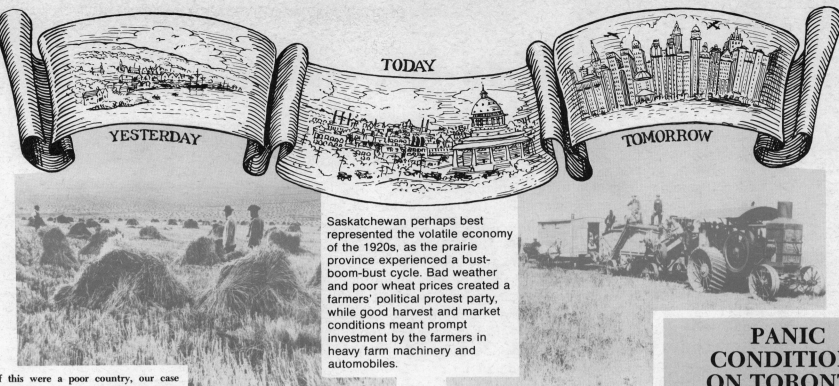

YESTERDAY TODAY TOMORROW

Saskatchewan perhaps best represented the volatile economy of the 1920s, as the prairie province experienced a bust-boom-bust cycle. Bad weather and poor wheat prices created a farmers' political protest party, while good harvest and market conditions meant prompt investment by the farmers in heavy farm machinery and automobiles.

The bountiful harvest of 1927: a wheatfield near Rockyford, Alberta

Threshers in Strathmore, Alberta, 1928

"If this were a poor country, our case would be a bad one, but we have riches in our forests, our fields, our fisheries and in our minerals; also in the mighty water powers and in the industry and ambition of our people."

PANIC CONDITIONS ON TORONTO MART

Uncertainty As Huge Blocks Sacrificed at New York

"SAFE" MARGINS WIPED OUT

TORONTO, Oct. 29—(Canadian Press Dispatch.)—The "market which could not come down" broke into a frenzied panic at this morning's opening in Wall Street following a steadily accelerating slump of weeks which had gathered alarming momentum in the last few days.

Men hurried along the streets in the cities of Canada and the United States, fearful, lips quivering, little knots formed in offices, with working discipline gone, as often-garbled versions of the break which could hardly be exaggerated flew around. The afternoon newspapers were besieged by telephone calls, and many of the voices at the other end, some feminine, were hysterical.

Word went around in Toronto that Nickel had dropped to 24, but this greatest Canadian mining issue did not go below 29 in the forenoon.

HUGE BLOCKS SACRIFICED
The New York break in the first half-hour was precipitate. As eager traders watched the tape, expecting an uncertain recovery, they saw, instead, huge blocks of sacrifice shares poured into the market, one after another, released by big operators who could no longer stand the pace. Rumours of brokerage failures were legion, and the first crystalized into fact when at about 11[a.m.] it was learned that the curb house of John I. Bell & Co. at New York had been suspended.

Yet optimism to some extent survived. The man on the street, in his hundreds of thousands, could be heard exclaiming "I wish I could buy so-and-so now at the bottom." But the bottom was constantly shifting. Housewives were using the telephones frantically, and a few heard and spread the word, and the telephone exchange reported heavy business.

With today's drastic drop there came into the wreckage ranks a large class of people who hitherto had been feeling quite comfortable—the large margin men, the 50 per centers, who in many cases saw margins of fondly imagined Gibraltar-like strength completely wiped out by the panic which had few equals in history.

London Free Press, Oct. 29, 1929

AN OLD MARITIMER

"While there were some automobiles in the village, we didn't have a car until much later on. Our family house had the basics, such as an outdoor privy and a good wood stove that handled the heating and cooking. Lord, we cut a lot of wood in those days. You see, back in the 1920s, there was no electrical power in our village. Most folks were just content with what they had. It was a good life. We wanted for nothing.

"Those younger folks that weren't so happy knew that whenever they wanted, they could move to a city and get a good paying job."

– from an interview

The Maritimes did not emerge from the slump of 1921-23, but seemed to settle into an almost chronic depression which severely curtailed development throughout the area.

T. Raddall, *Warden of the North*

MARKET DECLINE SEEN AS BENEFIT

"The recent slump has vividly demonstrated the instability of unparalleled returns in speculation by spending all available cash to purchase stock on margin. We may now confidently expect that people, sobered by this event, will use their money for tangibles such as home, health, and their comfort." Howard A. Lewis, Treasurer of Kelvinator of Canada Ltd. Nov. 1, 1929

FAMILY INCOME – 1929
Average = $1 900
Required = $2 200

Three generations of fishermen sort herring in the Grand Manan district, New Brunswick, July, 1920

Acknowledgements

The authors wish to acknowledge the Public Archives of Canada and the Ontario Public Archives as the principal source of photographs. We particularly appreciate the research assistance of Ginette Chatel of the Historic Photographs Section of the Public Archives.

In addition we are grateful to the contributions of Mr. Hans Anderson, J. H. Mattys, Mr. Earl Rosen, Mrs. Elvina Scaldwell, Mr. John Shier, Mrs. Bessie Slesser, Mr. Bryce Wiltsey, and Col. Harwood Steele. Other sources of original material include the Archives of Eaton's of Canada Limited, the Glenbow-Alberta Institute, the Football Hall of Fame, the Hockey Hall of Fame, Canada's Sports Hall of Fame, the London Public Library, the Weldon Library of the University of Western Ontario, and the Windsor *Star*. A word of thanks is due to Judith McErvel and Fay Wood of Eaton's Archives, and Linda Ervin of the Newspaper Section of the Public Archives of Canada for supplying materials for reproduction.

Finally, we wish to thank Rob Greenaway, Associate Editor, and Joan McCracken, Production Editor, both of Prentice-Hall, and William Fox, Designer for their assistance in producing this book.

Bibliography and Credits

PHOTOGRAPHS:

The authors and publisher would like to thank the following for providing materials for this text:

The abbreviations for the arrangement of photographs on each page are as follows: T=Top, M=Middle, B=Bottom, combined, when necessary with R=Right and L=Left. **p.2** T: Ontario Archives (OA) S 14323 **p.3** T: Public Archives of Canada (PAC) BH-42; **p.6** M: PAC PA-57700; **p.7** M: Glenbow-Alberta Institute (G-A) NA-1319-1; B: OA S 4822; **p.8** ML: PAC PA-50708 and Canada's Sports Hall of Fame; MR: PAC PA-88763; **p.9** T: OA RG 15; ML: OA 10103; MR: OA 10103; **p.12** T: PAC GL-90; ML: PAC C-20525; MR: PAC C-11477; BL: PAC PA-48656; **p.13** TL: PAC PA-44006; M: PAC GL-78; **p.14** T: PAC PA-43096; M: OA 9912; BL: PAC C-15169; **p.15** T: OA 10103; **p.16** T: PAC KJ-10; M: PAC PA-13012; **p.17** B: PAC PA-43089; **p.19** B: PAC PA-78962; others: private collection **p.20** TL: PAC BH-27; BL: PAC C-56705; **p.21** T: PAC C-26782; **p.22** T: PAC PA-54341; M: PAC PA-67269; B: PAC C-56793; **p.23** TL: PAC PA-54947; TR: OA 9912; ML: PAC PA-86634; **p.24** T: Alexandra Studios, 158 William St., Weston, Ont., and Canada's Sports Hall of Fame; MR: PAC PA-50440 and Canada's Sports Hall of Fame; BL: PAC PA-50296 and Canada's Sports Hall of Fame; BM: PAC PA-50338 and Alexandra Studios; BR: PAC PA-50307 and Canada's Sports Hall of Fame; **p.25** TL: PAC PA-30802; TM: PAC PA-50600, Alexandra Studios, and the Hockey Hall of Fame; TR: PAC PA-50277 and Canada's Sports Hall of Fame; M: Hamilton Football Hall of Fame; B: PAC PA-50465 and Canada's Sports Hall of Fame; **p.26** B: OA S 15000; **p.28** T: The Windsor *Star*; M: The Windsor *Star*; **p.29** TL: The Windsor *Star*; TR: The Windsor *Star*; **p.30** T: OA 9912; M: OA 9912; B: PAC C-7292; **p.31** T: PAC PA-31684; M: OA 9912; B: PAC PA 41242; **p.32** TL: PAC PA-54394; TM: PAC PA-96414; TR: PAC PA-86249; B: PAC PA-83988; **p.33** TL: PAC C-7471; TR: PAC DB-6; MR: PAC C-61657; BR: OA 9912; **p.34** T: PAC PA-19081; PAC PA-44509; **p.35** T: PAC PA-48683; M: G-A NA-1367-25; ML: PAC C-7140; MR: PAC PA-74612; B: PAC PA-88191; **p.36** T: PAC PA-31242; ML: PAC PA-41806; MR: PAC PA-43098; **p.37** R: PAC PA-20073; **p.38** T: PAC C-33357; M: PAC PA-84813; **p.39** TL: PAC C-36148; TR: OA 9912; B: PAC C-5849; **p.40** T: PAC PA-42982; B: OA S 15383; **p.41** T: PAC PA-95688; B: PAC PA-30784; **p.43** BL: PAC PA-18647; BR: PAC PA-48000; **p.44** M: OA S 2630; **p.45** M: PAC C-1690; **p.46** ML: OA 9912; BR: PAC PA-48767; **p.47** TL: PAC PA-40529; TR: PAC PA-40550; BL: PAC NFB FB33

Every reasonable effort has been made to find copyright holders of quotations. The publishers would be pleased to have any errors or omissions brought to their attention.

BOOKS AND CATALOGUES:

Allen, Richard. *The Social Passion: Religion and Social Reform in Canada, 1914-1928.* Toronto: University of Toronto Press, 1971.
Canada Year Book 1920-1931. Ottawa: Dominion Bureau of Statistics, 1920-1931.
Canadian Annual Review of Public Affairs 1928-29. Toronto: Annual Review Publishing Company, 1928-29.
Canadian Wage Rates and Hours of Labour 1901-1930. Ottawa: Department of Labour, 1901-1930.
Collins, Robert. *A Great Way To Go.* Toronto: McGraw-Hill Ryerson, 1969.
Cooper, John, Irwin. *Montreal: A Brief History.* Montreal: McGill-Queens University Press, 1969.
Donaldson, Gerald, and Lampert, Gerald, (eds.). *The Great Canadian Beer Book.* Toronto: McClelland and Stewart, 1976. Reprinted by permission of the Canadian Publishers, McClelland and Stewart Limited, Toronto.
Eaton's Catalogues, 1918-1929.
Eaton's News Weekly, 1924-1929.
Filey, Michael. *A Toronto Album: Glimpses of the City That Was.* Toronto: University of Toronto Press, 1970.
Furnas, J. C. *Great Times: An Informal History of the United States 1914-1929.* New York: G. P. Putnams and Sons, 1974.
Glazebrook, G. P. et al. *A Shopper's View of Canada's Past.* Toronto: University of Toronto Press, 1969.
Gray, James H. *The Roar of the Twenties.* Toronto: Macmillan Co. of Canada, 1975.
Hallowell, Gerald A. *Prohibition in Ontario 1919-23.* Toronto: Ontario Historical Society, 1972.
Hodgetts, A. B. *Decisive Decades.* Toronto: Thomas Nelson and Sons, 1960.
Hose, Reginald. *Prohibition or Control? Canada's Experience with the Liquor Problem 1921-27.* Toronto: Longmans, Green and Co., 1928.
Inglis, Alex. I. (ed.). *Documents on Canadian External Relations 1926-1930,* vol. 4. Ottawa: Department of External Affairs, 1967.
Johnston, W. V. *Before the Age of Miracles: Memoirs of a Country Doctor.* Toronto: Fitzhenry and Whiteside, 1972.
Keith, Ronald A., *Bush Pilot With A Briefcase: The Happy-Go-Lucky Story of Grant McConachie.* Toronto: Doubleday, 1972.
Labour Gazette, 1919-1925. Ottawa: Department of Labour, 1919-1925.
Labour Organizations in Canada 1924-26. Ottawa: Queen's Printer, 1924-26.
Ministry of Education, Province of Ontario. *Examination Papers,* 1919-1925.
Ministry of Education, Province of Ontario. *Teacher's Manual, History.*
Ontario Law Reform Commission. *Report on Sunday Observance Legislation.* Toronto: Ontario Department of Justice, 1970.

Rielly, Heather, and Handmarch, Marilyn. *Some Sources for Women's History in the Public Archives of Canada.* Ottawa: National Museums of Canada, 1974.
Spence, Ruth. *Prohibition in Canada.* Toronto: Ontario Branch of the Dominion Alliance, 1919.
Steele, Col. Harwood. *Policing the Arctic.* Toronto: Ryerson Press, 1935.
Stewart, Walter. *But Not in Canada.* Toronto: Macmillan of Canada Limited, 1976.
Stone, Larry. *Urban Development.* Ottawa: Queen's Printer, 1960.
Stone, Maud Morrison. *This Canada of Ours.* Toronto: The Musson Book Co. Ltd., 1929. Reprinted by permission of Hodder & Stoughton Limited, Toronto.
Treaties and Agreements Affecting Canada 1814-1925. Ottawa: Government of Canada, 1925.
Trofimenkoff, S. M., (ed.). *The Twenties in Western Canada.* Ottawa: History Division, National Museum of Man, 1972. Esp. John H. Thompson, "The Voice of Moderation: The Defeat of Prohibition in Manitoba", and William Calderwood, "Pulpit, Press, and Political Reactions to the Ku Klux Klan in Saskatchewan".
Weir, E. Austin. *The Struggle for National Broadcasting in Canada.* Toronto: McClelland and Stewart, 1965. Reprinted by permission of the Canadian Publishers, McClelland and Stewart Limited, Toronto.
Wise, S. F., and Fisher, Douglas. *Canada's Sporting Heroes.* Don Mills: General Publishing Co. Ltd., 1974

NEWSPAPERS AND PERIODICALS:

Canadian Aviation Magazine
The Chatelaine
Canadian Dimension, May, 1973
Everywoman's World, March, 1923
The Canadian Magazine
Toronto, *Globe*
Halifax Herald
Hamilton Spectator
The Herald (London, Ont.)
London Evening *Advertiser*
London Free Press
London Week-End *Mirror*
Maclean's Magazine
Manitoba *Free Press*
Montreal Daily *Star*
Ontario Secondary School Teachers' Federation *Bulletin* (now *Forum*)
The Regina *Leader-Post*
Saturday Night
Vancouver *Province*
Vancouver *Sun*
Winnipeg *Tribune*
Winnipeg *Free Press*